Petr Chadraba
Editor

The Central and Eastern European Markets: Guideline for New Business Ventures

Pre-publication
REVIEWS,
COMMENTARIES,
EVALUATIONS . . .

"What is different about this book is that through each of the different authors, it provides comparability between East European markets, description and commentary on Western strategies being deployed, and a depiction of potential market opportunities with a level of quantitative analysis which was not a feature of books on Eastern Europe before. The chapters are well written and not just sourced from the West either. It is interesting to see how the very first chapter deals with "Telecomms in the Tatras," underlining this very point. Previously, high tech sales to the Eastern bloc were not possible whereas now they are commonplace. The very institutions which were in place to constrain trade are now themselves gone. Now we are able to read assessments written by a Dean of a Czech Management Centre (Pendergast) and a manager in a high tech company such as Alcatel (Kreft), active now in the Czech Republic. That these names are not indigenous to the Czech Republic shows also the extent to which the Czech Republic is now open for business.

Information has always been sought of this part of the world but rarely found. In this book, we have a number of different contributions, each of which seeks to quantify the position in Eastern Europe by different means. Surveys of managers were not conducted previously. Response rates show that there is still a cultural problem with this form of information gathering but it is nevertheless pioneering research. These economies are still in transition and what this book can usefully do is to help interpret this area of the world neglected by Western investors. Bridgewater, McKiernan and Wensley have produced a well crafted insightful contribution which draws upon the existing international business literature as a framework for comparison to provide meaning to corporate behaviour, create typologies and identify

influences present in the market. Cox and Hooley have undertaken a survey of managers across Hungary, Poland and Bulgaria to highlight differences, respondents being asked to rank order factors which they believed key to competitor success. This has not been done before in this region of the world. We have to remind ourselves then of the fact that such things are relative innovations.

We are conscious today of the fact that these economies have undergone change but we must not forget it either because it reminds us where these economics have come from and helps us gauge their speed and direction towards the goal of attaining a free market economy, the ultimate measure of attractiveness for some corporate investors."

Stanley Paliwoda
Professor and Chair of Marketing at the University of Calgary, author of Investing in Eastern Europe *published 1995 by Addison Wesley/EIU Books, and Editor of the* Journal of East-West Business.

More pre-publication
REVIEWS, COMMENTARIES, EVALUATIONS . . .

"*T*he *Central and Eastern European Markets: Guideline for New Business Ventures* edited by Petr Chadraba is an interesting collection of strategies and approaches to rapidly evolving markets in Central and Eastern Europe. Since the political, social, and economic changes in 1989, these markets have experienced major transitions in their economic and business climates. Western managers need to understand issues such as the ones presented in this publication in order to successfully operate in these dynamic markets.

The most appropriate audience, however, is senior level students and graduate students in business and economics interested in Central and Eastern European operations. A number of international programs have begun to focus on the changes in this part of the world and are developing specific courses and seminars to address the emerging issues."

George Tesar, PhD
(International Marketing,
University of Wisconsin-Madison)
Professor of Marketing,
University of Wisconsin-Whitewater

The Central and Eastern European Markets: Guideline for New Business Ventures

The Central and Eastern European Markets: Guideline for New Business Ventures

Petr Chadraba
Editor

International Business Press
An Imprint of
The Haworth Press, Inc.
New York • London

Published by

International Business Press, 10 Alice Street, Binghamton, NY 13904-1580 USA

International Business Press is an imprint of The Haworth Press, Inc., 10 Alice Street, Binghamton, NY 13904-1580.

The Central and Eastern European Markets: Guideline for New Business Ventures has also been published as *Journal of East-West Business*, Volume 1, Number 3 1995.

Library of Congress Cataloging-in-Publication Data

The central and eastern European markets : guideline for new business ventures / Petr Chadraba, editor.
     p. cm.
     "Has also been published as Journal of East-West business, volume 1, number 3, 1995"–T.p. verso.
     Includes bibliographical references and index.
     ISBN 1-56024-712-6 (alk. paper)
     1. Investments, Foreign–Europe, Eastern. 2. Business enterprises, Foreign–Europe, Eastern. 3. New business enterprises–Europe, Eastern. 4. Europe, Eastern–Commerce. 5. Marketing–Europe, Eastern. I. Chadraba, Petr.
HF3500.7.Z5C46 1995
332.6'73'0947–dc20
                                            95-42395
                                                     CIP

INDEXING & ABSTRACTING

Contributions to this publication are selectively indexed or abstracted in print, electronic, online, or CD-ROM version(s) of the reference tools and information services listed below. This list is current as of the copyright date of this publication. See the end of this section for additional notes.

- *American Bibliography of Slavic and East European Studies (ABSEES) Compiled at the University of Illinois at Urbana-Champaign (246A Library, 1408 West Gregory Drive, Urbana, IL 61820) under the auspices of the American Association for the Advancement of Slavic Studies (Jordan Quad/Acacia Building, 125 Panama Street, Stanford, CA 94305-4130). Printed editions are published on an annual basis. Citations are also available in ABSEES Online, which can be accessed via the Internet (telnet to alexia.lis.uiuc.edu), or via dial-up connections (217-244-6451). At the "login:" prompt, type "absees"; at the "Password:" prompt, type "slavibib".* University of Illinois at Urbana-Champaign, 246A Library, 1408 West Gregory Drive, Urbana, IL 61801

- *Contents Pages in Management,* University of Manchester Business School, Booth Street West, Manchester M15 6PB, England

- *GEO Abstracts (GEO Abstracts/GEOBASE),* Elsevier/ GEO Abstracts, Regency House, 34 Duke Street, Norwich NR3 3AP, England

- *Guide to Social Science & Religion in Periodical Literature,* National Periodical Library, P.O. Box 3278, Clearwater, FL 34630

- *Human Resources Abstracts (HRA),* Sage Publications, Inc., 2455 Teller Road, Newbury Park, CA 91320

(continued)

- *Index to Periodical Articles Related to Law*, University of Texas, 727 East 26th Street, Austin, TX 78705

- *INTERNET ACCESS (& additional networks) Bulletin Board for libraries ("BUBL"), coverage of information resources on INTERNET, JANET, and other networks.*
  - JANET X.29: UK.AC.BATH.BUBL or 00006012101300
  - TELNET: BUBL.BATH.AC.UK or 138.38.32.45 login 'bubl'
  - Gopher: BUBL.BATH.AC.UK (138.32.32.45). Port 7070
  - World Wide Web: http: / / www.bubl.bath.ac.uk./BUBL/ home.html
  - NISSWAIS: telnetniss.ac.uk (for the NISS gateway)
  The Andersonian Library, Curran Building, 101 St. James Road, Glasgow G4 ONS, Scotland

- *Management & MarketingAbstracts,* Pira International, Randalls Road, Leatherhead, Surrey KT22 7RU, England

- *Operations Research/Management Science*, Executive Sciences Institute, 1005 Mississippi Avenue, Davenport, IA 52803

- *Political Science Abstracts*, IFI/Plenum Data Company, 3202 Kirkwood Highway, Wilmington, DE 19808

- *Referativnyi Zhurnal (Abstracts Journal of the Institute of Scientific Information of the Republic of Russia),* The Institute of Scientific Information, Baltijskaja ul., 14, Moscow A-219, Republic of Russia

- *Sociological Abstracts (SA),* Sociological Absracts, Inc, P.O. Box 22206, San Diego, CA 92192-0206

(continued)

SPECIAL BIBLIOGRAPHIC NOTES

related to special journal issues (separates)
and indexing/abstracting

☐ indexing/abstracting services in this list will also cover material in any "separate" that is co-published simultaneously with Haworth's special thematic journal issue or DocuSerial. Indexing/abstracting usually covers material at the article/chapter level.

☐ monographic co-editions are intended for either non-subscribers or libraries which intend to purchase a second copy for their circulating collections.

☐ monographic co-editions are reported to all jobbers/wholesalers/approval plans. The source journal is listed as the "series" to assist the prevention of duplicate purchasing in the same manner utilized for books-in-series.

☐ to facilitate user/access services all indexing/abstracting services are encouraged to utilize the co-indexing entry note indicated at the bottom of the first page of each article/chapter/contribution.

☐ this is intended to assist a library user of any reference tool (whether print, electronic, online, or CD-ROM) to locate the monographic version if the library has purchased this version but not a subscription to the source journal.

☐ individual articles/chapters in any Haworth publication are also available through the Haworth Document Delivery Services (HDDS).

ABOUT THE EDITOR

Dr. Petr Chadraba received his PhD in Business Administration from the University of Nebraska-Lincoln. Presently he is Associate Professor of Marketing at DePaul University, teaching International Marketing and Marketing Management. His current research interests are topics related to the application of Western business concepts in Central European economies. During the last three years, Dr. Chadraba developed and managed business education programs for managers of former state enterprises in Central Europe. He also works closely with several universities in the Czech Republic and Poland, helping them to develop undergraduate and graduate business curricula.

The Central and Eastern European Markets: Guideline for New Business Ventures

CONTENTS

Telecomms in the Tatras

William R. Pendergast
Klaus-Peter Kreft

THE INTERNATIONAL TENDER

Shortly after the "Velvet Revolution" of November 1989, the Czechoslovak government decided to upgrade the quality of its telecommunications system as an essential part of the infrastructure required for economic development. The federal government selected US West and DataCom to assist the Czechoslovak Post and Telecommunications Ministry (PTT) to design the specifications and requirements for modernization of the telecommunications system.

This review resulted in a 1990 International Tender for installation of a "digital overlay network" for public switching. All major international telecommunications companies submitted bids. After a six month evaluation, the PTT awarded the contract in May 1991 to Alcatel and Siemens.

The award guarantees each of the two companies, over the five-year period from 1991 to 1996, a minimum of 30% of the annual volume of PTT activity in the installation of the digital overlay public switching network. The remaining 40% of the business in this market is subject to annual competition. The business potential for each of the awardees therefore lies between 30 and 70 percent of the projected PTT market of

William R. Pendergast is Dean, Czechoslovak Management Center.
Klaus-Peter Kreft is Chairman, Alcatel Liptovsky Hradok.

This paper was prepared for presentation at a conference on "Strategies for Entering Eastern European Markets" in Vienna, November 25-26, 1993.

[Haworth co-indexing entry note]: "Telecomms in the Tatras." Pendergast, William R., and Klaus-Peter Kreft. Co-published simultaneously in *Journal of East-West Business* (International Business Press, an imprint of The Haworth Press, Inc.) Vol. 1, No. 3, 1995, pp. 1-16; and: *The Central and Eastern European Markets: Guideline for New Business Ventures* (ed: Petr Chadraba) International Business Press, an imprint of The Haworth Press, Inc., 1995, pp. 1-16. Single or multiple copies of this article are available from The Haworth Document Delivery Service [1-800-342-9678, 9:00 a.m. - 5:00 p.m. (EST)].

1

250,000 annual subscriber lines. At present, there are approximately 16 installed lines per 100 people in the two Republics. By the year 2000, they plan to reach a level of 32 lines per 100 persons, which is a level similar to Greece. Germany currently has 68 lines per 100 persons. The map of Czech and Slovak telephone districts is presented in Table 1.

Each of the two companies was thereby assured a significant share of an existing market and an opportunity to establish an extensive installed technological infrastructure that would constitute a substantial barrier to subsequent entry by other companies. It would be extremely difficult and costly for the PTT to change suppliers after the expiration in 1996 of the initial award.

The International Tender did not include a specific requirement that the awardee engage in a joint venture with a local company, but it did require local content. Alcatel SEL decided in favor of a joint venture and considered as candidates the two domestic manufacturers of public switching equipment. Each of these companies was part of the huge TESLA conglomerate: TESLA Liptovsky Hradok (TLH) in Slovakia and TESLA Karlin in the Czech Republic.

ALCATEL SEL

Headquartered in Stuttgart, West Germany, Standard Elektrik Lorenz AG (Alcatel SEL) is a major subsidiary of Alcatel n.v., the world's largest manufacturer of telecommunications products, including public switching systems, transmission systems, business systems, cables and cable systems. Alcatel SEL employs nearly 20,000 employees and achieves annual sales of some DM 6 billion in its seven divisions: Public Switching Systems, Line Transmission Systems, Radiocommunications, Business Systems, Defense and Aerospace, Transports and Components.

TESLA LIPTOVSKY HRADOK (TLH)

In 1991, TESLA Liptovsky Hradok (TLH) was a major telecommunications company with particular strength in private switching and a small line of public exchanges. It was founded in 1957 in the town of Liptovsky Hradok (Little Fortress of Liptov) and focused on the production of switches and switchboards supported by a license from a Canadian firm, Mitel Corporation. It employed some 2,500 persons and occupied 23,000 square meters of company premises in the scenic mountains of the

TABLE 1

Alcatel 1000 S 12

Alcatel SEL TLH a.s.: Telephone Districts in CR

ALCATEL
SEL TLH

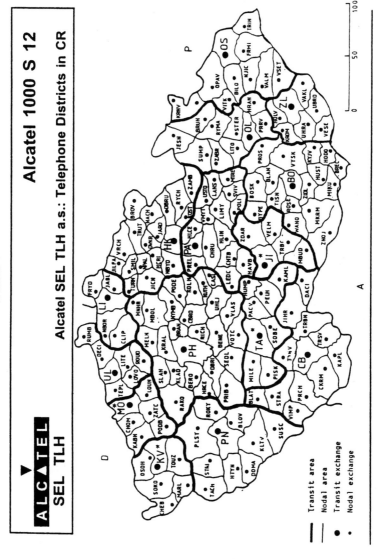

- | Transit area
- || Nodal area
- ● Transit exchange
- · Nodal exchange

TABLE 1 (continued)

Alcatel 1000 S 12

Alcatel SEL TLH a.s.: Telephone Districts in SR

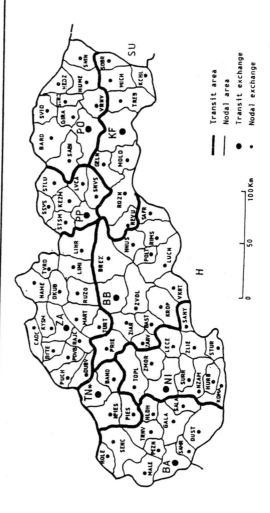

4

Low Tatra region of Slovakia. In 1980, TESLA became the first Czecho-slovakian company to manufacture electronic PABXs.

The mother firm, TESLA (abbreviation of technika slaboprouda or technology of low tension current), was a network of electric and electronic companies. In the 1980s it consisted of four divisions including 33 companies and 6 research institutes. It employed sixty to seventy thousand persons.

SEL SELECTS A PARTNER

The Alcatel decision to join with TLH symbolized its intention to create a self-contained, independent and autonomous unit–a separate and independent company. The major assets that the local partner could contribute to the joint venture would be physical facilities and personnel. The manufacturing facilities of TESLA Karlin, however, were integrally joined with other buildings and the business systems of the TESLA company. This made physical separation impractical, and it also raised concerns of security.

The cost of labor was also higher in the Prague area at Karlin, and would predictably become even higher in future years. Labor availability was more favorable in the Tatra region of Slovakia. Additionally, Siemens had been the original owner of TESLA Karlin, which raised the possibility of future restitution claims.

The joint venture with TESLA created an entirely new entity, Alcatel SEL (Standard Elektrik Lorenz) TLH (TESLA Liptovsky Hradok), or AST. The joint venture was founded on February 22, 1991 and registered on July 8, 1991. AST was an essential component of the bid that was submitted for the International Tender. SEL had 60 percent of the capital share and THL had 40 percent. Following the contract award in May 1991, reconstruction of the AST premises provided by TESLA in Liptovsky Hradok began in July 1991 and was completed in June 1992. Production started the same month, and AST opened officially on July 21, 1992. The key dates in the establishment of AST are presented in Table 2.

MOTIVES OF THE PARTIES

The partners in the joint venture clearly anticipated the benefits of a profitable commercial venture and the revenue that it would generate from its possible award in the International Tender. For Alcatel SEL, the new business promised to extend its international market share to Czechoslova-

TABLE 2

ALCATEL
SEL TLH

Alcatel 1000 S 12
Alcatel SEL TLH a.s.: Key Dates

- System Decision — May, 1991
- Registration AST — July 8, 1991
- Building Reconstruction
  - Start — July, 1991
  - Completion — June 1992
- Start Pilot-production (HW) — March, 1992
- Official Production Start — June, 1992
- Official Opening — July 21, 1992
- Start Training for O&M Alcatel 1000 S 12 — September, 1992
- Start Installation Alcatel 1000 S 12 — October, 1992
- Start CAE — November, 1992
- Start After Sales Services — April, 1993

kia and markets farther east. It would also provide an outlet for the sale of the printed board modules which it would continue to supply to AST from Stuttgart. The manufacture of these units was not only sensitive technology and therefore not available for transfer, but it required a production volume much larger than the prospective output of AST.

For TLH, the joint venture offered the opportunity to absorb redundant employees. TLH produced a significant line of high-technology military equipment, including military guidance systems. Military production in Czechoslovakia, however, did not face a bright future after the 1989 "velvet revolution." Since the joint venture planned eventually to acquire at least 50 percent of the value of its output from local sources (everything except the printed boards delivered from Alcatel SEL in Stuttgart), TESLA also welcomed the opportunity for its local metal workshop facilities to supply rack frames and other equipment to AST. Because of the independent status of AST, however, TLH could not anticipate any significant transfer of technology to its own benefit.

STRUCTURE OF THE JOINT VENTURE

The structure of AST gave Alcatel SEL a 60% interest, and 40% to TLH. In practice, the contributions of the parties consisted of: (1) an SEL cash investment of 12 million DM, product technology, and management know-how, and (2) a contribution of land and facilities by TLH that carried a valuation of 8 million DM.

Despite the fact that the forty percent TLH stake in the enterprise consisted of its contribution of land and plant, AST decided to completely gut the building and reconstruct it to a modern standard. This required an expenditure of 5 million DM, using local contractors to the greatest extent possible. Consequently, the forty percent TESLA stake in the enterprise included a generous allotment of "goodwill." This creation of a completely modern working environment was an important part of the cultural change that AST management wished to introduce in the workforce. It also had a significant customer relations impact. The actual reconstruction, however, and the employment of local contractors, provided a harsh introduction for Alcatel to the realities of operation in a culture where the supplier was king and the customer had to "mind his manners" to merit the privilege of service.

In addition to the 5 million DM reconstruction expenses, AST invested 16 million DM in machinery and equipment and 20 million DM in employee training and know-how transfer. The total value of the enterprise including the estimated value of the land and building, therefore, was nearly DM 50 million. This came from the contributions by the two parties, loans from German banks, supplier credit and cash flow from operations.

AST is managed on an operating basis by a five-person Management Board that includes three expatriate German employees and is chaired by the German General Manager, Klaus-Peter Kreft. All Management Board members have operational responsibilities at AST. The six-person Supervisory Board includes two representatives from Alcatel SEL, two from TESLA, and two from AST who are elected by AST employees, with a chairperson from TESLA. The AST management organization is presented in Table 3.

The AST operation includes an assembly plant, and a complete systems development software house. The plant produces Alcatel 1000 S 12 exchanges for public switching. It provides hardware production and testing, engineering (customer applications, training, and after-sales service), installation and operating support. It also produces transmission equipment and main power supply equipment for Alcatel 1000 S12 and other applications in public switching. The anticipated single-shift annual production volume of Alcatel 1000 S12 is 270,000 terminations and 400 power supply units. With little investment, this capacity could be tripled by additional shifts and building expansion. The AST product line is presented in Table 4.

DEALING WITH UNCERTAINTIES

In entering this business venture, the partners faced several uncertainties. These included: (1) recruitment and training of qualified and motivated employees, (2) the market potential both within and outside Czechoslovakia, particularly since customer financing depended on international lending agencies, and (3) political uncertainties at the future development and stability of the new government regime.

Staffing the Enterprise

As a new, "greenfield" venture, AST did not assume the accumulated burden of existing employees that occurs when western companies acquire local manufacturing enterprises. At the same time, only three German employees in key positions were to work at AST. These were Klaus-Peter Kreft, the Technical Director and Chairman of the Management Board, Rainer Rotzoll in Finance and Control, and Pieter Caron in Engineering and Logistics.

TABLE 3

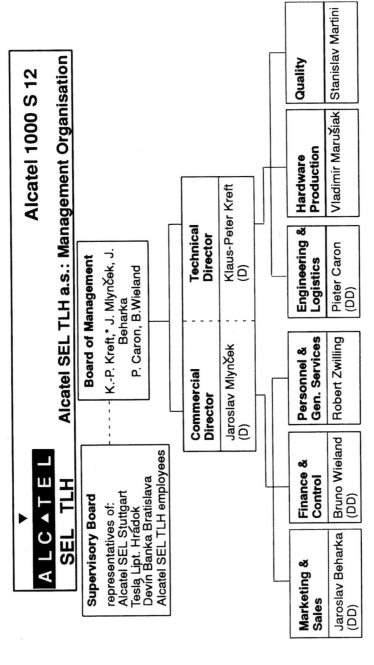

Alcatel 1000 S 12

Alcatel SEL TLH a.s.: Management Organisation

ALCATEL SEL TLH

Supervisory Board

representatives of:
Alcatel SEL Stuttgart
Tesla Lipt. Hrádok
Devin Banka Bratislava
Alcatel SEL TLH employees

Board of Management

K.-P. Kreft,* J. Mlynček, J. Beharka
P. Caron, B.Wieland

Commercial Director

Jaroslav Mlynček
(D)

Technical Director

Klaus-Peter Kreft
(D)

Marketing & Sales

Jaroslav Beharka
(DD)

Finance & Control

Bruno Wieland
(DD)

Personnel & Gen. Services

Robert Zwilling

Engineering & Logistics

Pieter Caron
(DD)

Hardware Production

Vladimir Marušiak

Quality

Stanislav Martini

* Chairman of the Board of Management
(D) Director
(DD) Deputy Director

9

TABLE 4

ALCATEL
SEL TLH

Alcatel 1000 S 12
Alcatel SEL TLH a.s.: Products

Alcatel 1000 S 12 Exchanges for Public Switching

* Hardware Production and Test
* Engineering
  - Customer Application Engineering
  - SLT - Production
  - Customer Training
  - After Sales Service
* Installation and Operating Support

Transmission Equipment (1. Order)

Main Power Equipment for Alcatel 1000 S 12
(Czech Republic, Slovak Republic, Export)

* Hardware Production and Test

The Production of other Telecommunication Products is foreseen.

AST had the challenge and the advantage, therefore, of recruiting and training an entirely new staff of managerial and technical employees. Fortunately, it had a potential source of such employees in its TLH partner. Since the AST Commercial Director, Jaroslav Mlyncek, was a native of the region and a former TLH employee, AST was able to "cherrypick" promising and able employees from TLH and the region. It found that there was no shortage of technically qualified employees in the area.

AST employs approximately 350 persons, about half of whom are engineers. Training for these new employees and technical support for them were an initial priority. In the first year, 112 trainees were sent to Stuttgart for a total of 1695 manweeks of training in production of System 12 and main power equipment, engineering, installation and administration. In addition, there were 800 manweeks of technical support from SEL, on site at TLH. Initially, therefore, AST placed the emphasis on technical training of production employees. The training and technical support scheme is presented in Table 5.

In personnel matters, the two most difficult challenges were language deficiencies and employee attitudes and work culture. Language was a barrier to both technical and managerial training. Despite the German origins of Alcatel SEL, AST selected English as its second internal language. The limited foreign language proficiency of the local population, however, severely restricted the number of people to whom technical knowledge could be transferred.

Culturally, AST faced the challenge to instill in employees a western work ethic and conception of the business. It was a radical shift, for example, to convince production-oriented employees that the true AST product is not so much hardware, but software and service.

In its initial recruitment, AST attempted to screen applicants based on their attitudes and predispositions by interviews and the administration of language and technical tests. It did not employ psychological testing.

AST provides employees a base salary that is twenty percent above local standards, and a performance supplement that may add up to 40 percent of base salary. There is also the possibility to earn a premium for exceptional individual performance, as well as a bonus based on overall company results. This combination of compensation elements provides a significant advantage to working at AST and also creates incentives for both individual performance and teamwork.

Employees at AST established a system of elected "speakers" who represent company employees to management. At an early stage in AST operation, there was talk of establishing a union. AST management argued successfully that it made little sense to link their own fortunes to those of

TABLE 5

Alcatel 1000 S 12

ALCATEL
SEL TLH

Alcatel SEL TLH a.s.: Training/Technical Support

	Training		Technical Support	
	Number of Trainees	Training in Manweeks	Number of Functions	Effort in Manweeks
S 12 Production	32	230	9	248
MPE Production	5	20	2	20
Engineering	33	1,053	5	256
Installation	40	385	2	276
Administration	2	7	0	0
Total	112	1,695	18	800

completely disparate enterprises like antiquated steel firms located a great distance away.

Political Uncertainties

Following the separation of the Czech and Slovak Republics, the Czech and Slovak governments continued the agreement concluded by the former Czechoslovak PTT. Although neither of the partners anticipated separation, it turned out to be a strategic advantage for Alcatel to be located in Slovakia. This conferred prominence in the Slovak marketplace while marketing links in the Czech Republic were not difficult to assure. Had both Siemens and AST been situated in either the Czech or Slovak Republic, they would have been vulnerable to competitive entry by a third party competitor into the other Republic. Following separation, SEL opened a branch office in Prague where installation and testing and after-sales service for the Czech Republic can be assured.

Market Potential

AST did not plan to confine its activities to the 30-70 percent of the public switching market in Czechoslovakia that was awarded in the international tender. The partners intended to establish by 1993 a profitable home base in the domestic market for public switching. In 1994, AST would be in a position to penetrate the broader Russian and East European markets in public switching and also to expand its market to new products and new customers within the domestic area. This ambitious goal was a principal reason why the partners decided to establish AST as an autonomous unit rather than simply a "workbench" in a larger, integrated production system to serve the domestic market. The existence of an internal system house at AST, for example, gives it the strategic and operational flexibility to develop new markets and products.

AST is configured to be a profitable concern with 50 percent of the public switching market in the Czech and Slovak Republics. Activities beyond that level become an attractive extension but are not essential to the profitability of the firm. In the initial phase of the modernization program, Czechoslovak PTTs intended to purchase 180,000 terminations, compared with the planned AST output of 270,000 terminations.

The Russian and East European markets were a natural objective for expanded AST activities. Once AST production was established and serving the domestic Czech and Slovak markets at a profitable level, it would provide a low-cost platform for exports to the East. In addition, AST personnel at Liptovsky Hradok shared cultural and linguistic affinities with other Slavic regions that could provide a significant competitive advantage. In fact, this latter aspect of AST provides a capability that is used advantageously by other Alcatel divisions.

The AST market in the switching field is confined to the public domain. This includes the PTTs but also other public entities such as railroads and government ministries. Alcatel Business Systems handles sales and service of switching equipment to private enterprises. In addition to public switching equipment, however, AST also produces power generation and transmission equipment which it can sell to both public and private sectors.

New market prospects for ASP, therefore, include: (1) new clients for existing products (e.g., power supply units for enterprises outside the telecommunications industry), (2) product extensions of existing public switching systems (e.g., special networks for the military), and (3) complementary but entirely new products (e.g., high voltage power distribution equipment) in which there would be production synergies.

LESSONS AND STRATEGIES

By Autumn 1993, AST management was in a position to look back on its two years of activity and reflect on its experiences and lessons, and to consider its future strategies and the decisions they would require. The practical experience and lessons learned by AST appear in Table 6.

Lessons Learned

Many western investments in Central Europe commence with a western partner acquiring a controlling interest in a local company with an established market for its products. Buying market share is a common motive for western companies that acquire local enterprises in Central Europe. AST also entered existence as a joint venture with an assured market, albeit through the different mechanism of a government contract award. Because of the need for a quick start, such an assured market provides a solid base for new enterprise.

A greenfield investment has the advantage of avoiding the accumulated baggage of the past: obsolete facilities and equipment, antiquated processes and policies, and ingrained behaviors and attitudes. It provides an opportunity for a fresh start.

Besides the language barrier, culture and work ethic was the most difficult human resource issue for AST. Technical training was straightfor-

TABLE 6

ALCATEL
SEL TLH

Alcatel 1000 S 12

Alcatel SEL TLH a.s.: Practical Experience

- Qualified people for "High-Tech" working places are available
- Language problems reduced the amount of people to which "Know-How" can be transferred
- Missing "Know-How" about modern management techniques requires a broad spectrum of training
- Highly motivated people allow fast realization of projects
- Inadequate taxation system
- Financing restrictions

15

ward and found a receptive environment and an educated workforce. Issues of teamwork, responsibility, task completion, initiative and creativity, and communication are more intractable matters.

Future Strategies

AST had secured its base objective by Autumn 1993. With an expected 1994 turnover of 60-65 million DM, it was operating at a profitable level of activity and had a solid domestic market for its core product. AST management needed to consider its next steps and alternatives.

Which segment of the domestic market should it address next? Should it extend its switching business to specialized public markets? Should it develop markets for its power supply units? Should it expand its products into new but related areas? What is the potential of each of these alternative markets? What is the nature of competition in them? What additional resources will they require? How should AST address foreign markets? How does AST and its export strategy fit into overall Alcatel and TESLA strategy?

Strategic Investment Decisions by Western Firms in Ukraine: The Role of Relationships in Home and Host Market Networks

Sue Bridgewater
Peter McKiernan
Robin Wensley

SUMMARY. The transition to free market economy in Ukraine has resulted in the country entering a period of discontinuous change. Much of the necessary infrastructure for a free market economy is missing. Enforced segregation from the rest of the developed world has resulted in inherently different socio-cultural beliefs. The economy is in crisis. There is a lack of reliable statistical data, invalidating the use of traditional matrix-based planning tools. Yet there has been a significant level of Western investment in Ukraine since liberalisation. In many instances, this has involved "high commitment" modes of operation (Johanson and Vahlne 1977).

Research into international entry and expansion decisions from macro-economic, strategic, behavioural and marketing perspectives differs as to the relative weight which it accords to exogenous and endogenous influences. However, a recurrent theme is that uncertainty increases risk. Traditional "stage" models of internationalisa-

Sue Bridgewater is affiliated with Warwick Business School, Coventry, England.
Peter McKiernan is affiliated with the University of St. Andrews, Scotland.
Robin Wensley is affiliated with Warwick Business School, Coventry, England.

[Haworth co-indexing entry note]: "Strategic Investment Decisions by Western Firms in Ukraine: The Role of Relationships in Home and Host Market Networks." Bridgewater, Sue, Peter McKiernan, and Robin Wensley. Co-published simultaneously in *Journal of East-West Business* (International Business Press, an imprint of The Haworth Press, Inc.) Vol. 1, No. 3, 1995, pp. 17-35; and: *The Central and Eastern European Markets: Guideline for New Business Ventures* (ed: Petr Chadraba) International Business Press, an imprint of The Haworth Press, Inc., 1995, pp. 17-35. Single or multiple copies of this article are available from The Haworth Document Delivery Service [1-800-342-9678, 9:00 a.m. - 5:00 p.m. (EST)].

17

tion would suggest that the level and nature of foreign investment in Ukraine is counter-intuitive, given the levels of uncertainty. This paper explores the entry and expansion decisions which Western firms are making in Ukraine. It seeks to understand why firms make "high commitment" investments in markets in transition. Moreover, it looks at the ways in which firms use relationships in the home and host market to reduce the risks of strategic investment decisions in Ukraine. *[Article copies available from The Haworth Document Delivery Service: 1-800-342-9678.]*

1. THE UKRAINIAN CONTEXT

1.1 Transition to a Free Market Economy

The process of transition in East and Central Europe is one which is unique. Parallels have been drawn with the period of regeneration and rebuilding after the second world war. However, there are key differences. East and Central Europe have been artificially segregated from the rest of the developed world for more than a generation. The current process is not one of regeneration, but of generation of the requisite infrastructure for a free market economy. Moreover, many of the procedures and attitudes required to make the transition are socio-culturally alien.

The levels of macro-environmental uncertainty in the Ukraine are exceptionally high, even by the standards of East and Central Europe. A fierce urge to be independent has led Ukraine to divorce itself, many say prematurely, from the "rouble-zone." The large, state-owned enterprises have lost their former Soviet markets. The temporary currency, the "Karbovanet" or coupon, is not convertible and the introduction of the proposed new currency, the Griyivnya, has been repeatedly postponed (Central European 1993). Ukraine is currently suffering from hyper-inflation; more than 50% per month and accelerating. *The Economist* (23rd October 1993) quotes an inflation rate of more than 70% in the month of September and an aggregate rate of 5200% per annum. Foreign investors and Ukrainian citizens are united in the view that conditions have become more difficult in the last 12 months.

This worsening situation was predicted. Oleksander Savchenko, Director of the Centre for Advanced Economic Studies in Kiev, suggested in November 1992 (Central European) that inflation would reach 60-70% per month because the budget deficit is currently being financed by printing more money.

Manninen and Snelbecker (1993) attribute the worsening situation to the process of transition:

One of the several important differences between Ukraine today and Ukraine six and twelve months ago is that Ukraine is now far deeper into the transition process than it was then. Old governmental command-control structures and institutional relationships have disintegrated to a far greater degree now than they had then, creating confusion and disorder (. . .) It may be tempting to conclude (. . .) that the best way for Ukraine to improve its business climate would be to return to the period of stability of last year. This conclusion would be a mistake (. . .) a more prudent policy would be to move forward swiftly and decisively, through the current transition period.

A worrying question is the level of governmental commitment to reform. Volodomyr Griniov, once Deputy Chairman of the Ukrainian Parliament, now leader of "Nova Ukraina," a non-governmental centrist association (*Privatisation in Ukraine* June/July 1993) stresses the need to strive towards the goal of free market economy despite the current economic crisis.

However, time passes without the necessary steps being taken. Griniov admits that 6 months have been wasted in the privatisation process. *The Economist* takes a more pessimistic view (23rd October 1993). It lauds the bloodless resolution of the political problems in Ukraine, but questions the will to change. Many key government positions are still held by former Communist party members. Manninen and Snelbecker (1993) propose a number of measures essential to improvement of the climate for foreign investment in Ukraine:

- The creation of a legal infrastructure to support and protect private enterprise
- Rapid small-scale privatisation to provide capital and expertise to a new class of Ukrainian business people
- The creation of a stable, convertible currency and a commercial banking sector to give people access to capital and financial services
- Price liberalisation
- Demonopolisation of large amalgamates into smaller units
- Subsequent privatisation of these enterprises to create an economy of private, competitive enterprises.

1.2 Foreign Investment in Ukraine

The level of investment in Ukraine lags behind that of other East and Central European countries. A survey of 400 medium-sized Western firms carried out by Deloitte Touche Tohmatsu (12-10-92) investigates the interest in investment in various Eastern European countries. Degree of interest (in percentage terms) is shown in Table 1.

Ukraine's inclusion in the survey, alongside Russia, implies that it is attractive to investors. The omission of Kazakhstan is interesting, as oil exploration has led to significant investment activity. Ukraine performs relatively badly in the survey. This almost certainly reflects its slow rate of transition. The Visegrad countries have clearly made more decisive steps forward. The proximity of Ukraine to Russia may also be a factor, as this continues to cause anxiety. Ukraine, like Czech Republic, is dependent for domestic and industrial purposes upon oil supplies from Russia. There are questions as to the likelihood of these supplies continuing, given the changed relationship between the countries. Also, these supplies are currently priced at less than world price, a situation which is not predicted to continue (*Prognosis* October 15th 1993). Moreover, the recent attempted coup in Russia emphasised the vulnerability of Ukraine. A recent survey of the issues which Ukrainian people see as important (U.S. Information Agency 1992) shows that their major fear is possible attack by a third party, probably Russia.

Yet, despite the problems of day-to-day operation in Ukraine and the worsening conditions, there has still been a significant level of Western investment. The majority of investments have taken place since the break-up of the former Soviet Union, although a small number had been initiated before. Figures vary according to the source. The Ukrainian business weekly, *Torgovaya Gazeta* (June 1993), lists more than 800 joint ventures in Ukraine, of which 578 are in Kiev, 82 in Odessa, 72 in Lvov and 51 in Donetsk. More than 50% of these are in Business Services/Trading and only 16% in production. However, Izvestia lists 3,380 foreign investments

TABLE 1

	Hung.	Pol.	CSFR	Russ.	Ukr.	Romania
Austria	74	61	74	52	39	39
Denmark	52	76	48	36	6	6
France	48	40	52	36	36	20
Germany	65	65	71	65	41	35
Japan	40	10	10	20	0	10
Nor/Swe/Fin	33	55	33	78	28	11
UK	53	47	53	35	23	29
USA/Can	53	53	53	63	33	21

in Ukraine during 1992, which does not include 366 companies from 45 countries with registered offices in Ukraine.

2. CONCEPTUAL BACKGROUND

2.1 Entry and Expansion Decisions in Markets in Transition

International investment decisions have been researched from a number of different disciplinary perspectives. Buckley (1991) identifies a continuum of research ranging from economic analyses, which see decisions as externally-dictated by market imperfections, to strategic analyses, which recognize the role of managerial discretion. Hence, the relative importance which research attaches to exogenous and endogenous influences upon decisions spans a wide spectrum of views.

Despite this apparent polarity, a central tenet of research into decision-making is that high levels of uncertainty increase the risk of the decision. Economic analyses view uncertainty as a cause of increased transaction costs (Williamson 1975). High levels of psychic distance are held by behavioural research to be an inhibitor of international investment decisions (Johanson and Wiedersheim-Paul 1975; Johanson and Vahlne 1977). Research into strategic decision-making identifies uncertainty as a key contributor to the perceived risk of a decision (Hickson et al. 1985).

Uncertainty in the Ukrainian market is comprised of a number of factors. Firstly, segregation from the rest of the developed world has resulted in a distinctly different environment. Secondly, the duration of the current period of transition is difficult to predict. Thirdly, the composition of uncertainty is difficult to ascertain. It is comprised of a large number of variables. Many of the variables are inter-related. The rapidity of change has resulted in there being little reliable statistical data which has invalidated the use of matrix-based planning tools to assess the risk of operation in the market. Moreover, many contributory factors, such as psychic distance and the socio-cultural impact of the totalitarian régime, cannot be measured by hard quantitative techniques.

Hence, high levels of uncertainty in Ukraine seem to pose significant risk to potential investors. Moreover, the precise nature of those risks is difficult to ascertain. The current pattern of investment by firms in "high commitment" seems, intuitively, to be hard to reconcile with the literature.

2.2 Traditional Models of Internationalisation

Traditional, incremental models of internationalisation (Johanson and Wiedersheim-Paul 1975; Johanson and Vahlne 1977) contend that firms' export and expansion decisions are inhibited by lack of knowledge and experience of foreign markets. High levels of uncertainty, which must be overcome when entering new geographic markets, will result in the adoption of lower-commitment modes of operation. As the firm increases its knowledge of a market, it will increase its commitment to it.

Despite its widespread use, the incremental model has fundamental limitations. Although empirically proven for stable, industrialised countries (Johanson and Wiedersheim-Paul 1975; Dichtl et al. 1984), the model has been found to be invalid in a number of other situations (Turnbull 1987; Erramilli 1990; Clark and Mallory 1992). Empirical evidence exists to suggest that firms do not follow a uni-directional process (Jatar 1992). Firms may follow different patterns of entry and expansion in accordance with their strategic intent in operating in the market. Moreover, there is debate as to what constitutes the discrete stages, and, indeed, as to what should be the first, or lowest commitment, type of operation (Turnbull 1987; Erramilli 1990).

Johanson and Vahlne (1990) acknowledge that the explanatory power of the model is partial. Larger steps in the internationalisation process may be made if the firm has high levels of resources. High levels of international experience facilitate generalization between similar markets (Forsgren 1989). The model is not always applicable for service industries (Erramilli and Rau 1990, Johanson and Sharma 1987).

More importantly, however, the basis of the model is fundamentally flawed. Penrose (1959) identifies two types of knowledge: experiential, which cannot be transferred, and objective, which can be taught. Johanson and Vahlne (1977) contend that the knowledge required to overcome market uncertainty must be experiential and market specific. However, the recent nature of transition in Ukraine is such that few have direct market specific knowledge. Moreover, the climate changes with a rapidity that invalidates yesterday's knowledge. Nonetheless, Western firms are entering and expanding in the market via joint ventures or by investment in greenfield operations. Hence, it seems that the process model is of limited value in understanding investment decisions which are being made in Ukraine.

2.3 The Role of Networks of Relationships

One of the ways in which firms may be overcoming the uncertainty of investment in Ukraine is by means of information gained via existing relationships. Thus, in this context, the network paradigm may offer a valuable contribution to understanding of entry and expansion decisions.

A network is defined by Håkansson and Johanson (1992) as a set of relationships, whereby actors gain access to scarce resources. A relationship tends to be formed where there is asymmetry of resources and actors perceive mutual benefit in some form of exchange.

Networks may involve many types of exchange relationship. Thorelli (1986) sees flows of "power and information" in the network as being more significant than economic exchange. In the context of Ukraine, information is a scarce resource which may be exchanged via network relationships. Market-entry decisions may be influenced by other actors with whom the firm has a relationship (Johanson and Vahlne 1990; Johanson and Mattsson 1988) (see Figure 1). This view is supported by the findings of Johanson and Sharma (1987) in relation to small, technical consultancy firms. Thus, the network view is that entry and expansion decisions are more greatly influenced by relationships with customers, competitors and other stakeholders in the market, than by country-specific variables or levels of environmental uncertainty (Figure 1).

2.4 Relationships and Information Flows in Markets in Transition

One of the interesting questions in researching markets in transition from a network perspective is whether there are networks of relationships. In Western economies an organization has direct relationships with its suppliers and customers and indirect relationships with a larger sphere of stakeholders. A considerable body of marketing literature is devoted to the nature and effectiveness of interaction between channel members (Håkansson and Wootz 1975a, 1975b; Lusch 1976; Etgar 1978) A significant contribution in this field has been made by the work of the International Marketing and Purchasing Group (Turnbull and Valla 1986; Håkansson 1982; Young and Wilkinson 1989).

However, there is considerable debate as to the nature, and indeed the existence of channel relationships in markets in transition (De Wit and Monami 1993; Pyatt 1993; Tesar 1993; Mattsson 1993). The economic

FIGURE 1

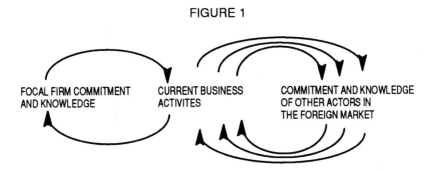

| FOCAL FIRM COMMITMENT AND KNOWLEDGE | CURRENT BUSINESS ACTIVITES | COMMITMENT AND KNOWLEDGE OF OTHER ACTORS IN THE FOREIGN MARKET |

system in former COMECON countries was driven by a central plan where production output was used to measure compliance and performance. Theoretically, and in some cases realistically, firms did not know the final customers or what the products were going to be used for. Mattsson (1993) describes markets in transition as having "arm's length transactions between 'faceless' sellers and buyers." In this situation, the link between buyers and sellers is, at least, less direct or, at its most extreme, not an exchange relationship. The real exchange would be between the producer and the government.

A key implication of this debate for Western firms assessing the attractiveness of entry into markets in transition is that the difference in network structures further hinders information flow. This compounds the problems associated with reliable evaluation of the potential of investment opportunities.

3. RESEARCH PROPOSITIONS

This research aims:

1. To explore, in context, the entry and expansion decisions of Western firms in Ukraine.
2. To gain a better understanding of why firms opt for "high commitment" modes of operation in Ukraine.
3. To examine the existence and nature of exchange relationships in Ukraine.
4. To identify why firms make these decisions.

4. METHODOLOGY

4.1 Choice of Methodology

The exploratory nature of this research influences the choice of methodology. Harrigan (1983) emphasises the value of "fine-grained," qualitative methodologies for the exploration of "nuances and complexity." Thus, fine-grained methodologies are seen to be applicable for this complex, inter-disciplinary area. A case-based methodology is preferred, as this allows for consideration of entry and expansion decisions in their context. Moreover, Harrigan emphasises the value of cases as means of capturing "the complexities of corporate strategy, competition and uncontrollable environmental factors surrounding strategy formulation." Case studies do not allow for broader generalization of findings. However, "coarse-grained" analyses would not offer a full understanding of the multiplex influences upon entry and expansion decisions.

4.2 Sampling and Data Collection

Where possible, data for the case studies have been collected both in the Ukraine and in the Western operation. Secondary data at firm and industry level have been referenced, where appropriate. Thus, cases are validated by use of multiple sources of evidence (Yin 1983).

Cases were drawn from the Accountancy, Chemical, Household Goods and Tobacco Industries as these sectors showed a high level of investment activity in Ukraine and represent a range of consumer and industrial, product and service industries. Semi-structured interviews were used for data-collection to avoid the inhibiting influence of the pursuit of "closure" (Egan 1993).

Issues which were explored in interviews were:

Firm-Specific Variables: Firm size, Ownership; Organizational Structure; Level of international experience; Experience of operation in other Eastern European markets; Current mode of operation in Ukraine; Current mode of operation in other Eastern European markets.

Country-Specific Variables: What are perceived to be the major risks and opportunities of operation in Ukraine; What sources of information are to make investment decisions and to operate in Ukraine; Who are the key stakeholders in the market.

Strategic Variables: Process of entry into Ukraine; Strategic objective for operation in Ukraine; Reason for choice of this type of operation; Sources of influence in decision; Sources of information used in decision to enter Ukraine; Process of decision-making; Criteria against which success of operation is measured; Timescale for assessment of success; Criteria on which a further investment would be made.

Data were analysed at firm and industry level to identify similarities and differences. From this analysis, a number of groups of firms were found that exhibited broadly similar types of behaviour.

5. TYPOLOGIES OF STRATEGIC BEHAVIOUR

Within an industry, firms may adopt different competitive strategies. A number of attempts have been made to classify these into categories. Porter (1985) identifies differentiation, cost leadership and focus as "generic" strategies. Miles and Snow (1986) identify a number of typologies of firm behaviour: Prospectors, who are innovators; Analyzers, who refine upon the ideas of others; Defenders, who are essentially followers; and those who use Dynamic Networks to gain flexibility in conditions of discontinuous change. The critical variable in arriving at these typologies is the lifecycle stage of the industry.

Building upon this categorisation, all the firms who currently operate in the Ukraine are innovators, in that they are early entrants into a high-risk market. However, the industry sectors from which cases are drawn are all, broadly-speaking, mature. Using the Miles and Snow typology these firms would tend to be either Analysers or Defenders. Yet, the turbulent market environment has also led to a number of firms exhibiting behaviour which seems more characteristic of Prospectors or Dynamic Networks.

It appears that the Miles and Snow typologies cannot adequately explain the decision-making behaviour of firms in Ukraine. Preliminary analysis of data allows identification of a number of broad groupings which exhibit distinct patterns of behaviour.

5.1 Option-Takers are attracted by market potential. They take a nominal investment in order to assess the prospects in the market. It is likely that this represents the first move towards a higher level of investment in the future.

5.2 First-Movers have invested in market via a "high-commitment" mode of operation, such as a Manufacturing Joint Venture. The risk of this choice is seen to be justified in the long-term by the potential benefits of first-mover advantage.

5.3 Client-Followers follow global customers into the market. The risk of commitment is partially offset by guaranteed business with existing customers and is seen to be justified in terms of developing the customer relationship.

5.4 Deal-Makers are similarly influenced by existing relationships. The decision to invest is based upon guaranteed funding from the government or other agencies.

While there are clear links between the type of industry and strategic choices, there are some overlaps. This suggests that it is not industry sector, but rather whether the firm serves industrial or consumer markets which is a key variable.

6. INFLUENCES UPON STRATEGIC INVESTMENT DECISIONS

Figure 2 shows the patterns of influences on the investment decisions of each group. This is mapped on Achrol, Reve and Stern's diagram of the task environment surrounding the firm (1985). The environment in which the firm operates is split into vertical environment (inputs and outputs) and lateral environment (influence groups and competitors).

Client-Followers are most influenced by their industrial customers (output environment). These customers may be First-Movers.

Deal-Makers are most influenced by links with funding bodies in the lateral, regulatory environment. Subsequent business is sought after the initial investment in the market. This may be via links in the regulatory environment or else with first-movers in the market.

First-Movers are influenced by market potential (output environment). They are also motivated by the actions of their rivals (competitive environment). These firms tended to be found in highly competitive oligopolies. The primary aim is to establish defensible market-share before competitors.

Option-Takers are also influenced by market potential. Like first-movers, they are very concerned about the actions of their oligopolistic rivals. However, they adopt a more cautious approach to investment. Further investment is likely, but they are currently assessing market potential in greater detail.

7. SOURCES OF INFORMATION USED IN INVESTMENT DECISIONS

7.1 Secondary Sources of Data

Reliable statistical data is difficult to obtain in Ukraine. The rapidity of transition often renders it invalid on publication. The secrecy in which sources of information have historically been veiled makes verification problematic. Consequently, contradictory information can be difficult to reconcile. All of those interviewed recommended cross-referencing of multiple sources of data. Some key sources of secondary data which are currently used are:

  i. Local Press. Information can be contradictory and suffers from the aforementioned problems of validation. However, many legislative decrees are first published in local press.
 ii. Foreign Press and Business Periodicals, e.g.: *Financial Times, Wall Street Journal, Economist's Business Central Europe*. Western interviewees placed more credence on data obtained from Western Sources but noted that coverage is limited.
iii. Official Statistics. Some information is available in the public domain, such as output figures and location of enterprises. However,

key pieces of information seem to be unobtainable from these sources. One respondent described the process of data-collection as one of interdependent loops wherein vital links seem to be missing.
iv. Former-Soviet Electronic Databases. They are paid services and are centrally-administered. The accuracy of data from these sources has not been ascertained.

7.2 Primary Sources of Data

A key social impact of transition in Ukraine is the resultant change in employment patterns. Such is the disparity between hard and soft currency values, that senior professionals with language skills often leave their previous employ to work as interpreters and facilitators for Western business. Accordingly, many of the local employees of Western firms in Ukraine combine high levels of specialism with good local knowledge. Preliminary indications suggest that local networks are in existence, although these may be different to Western equivalents. Ukrainian employees can provide a bridge into local networks.

Business Schools are demonstrably at the forefront of management expertise in many areas. For this reason, staff often provide consultancy services. Market research is key amongst these. Additionally, Ukrainian students working on study-related projects may offer an additional means of accessing data.

A number of Western and Ukrainian market research agencies are now in existence. One interviewee expressed concern that the current economic situation can make Western prices unaffordable for firms operating in the local currency. However, it is to be hoped that this is a temporary impact of transition.

7.3 Sources of Information Used in Strategic Investment Decisions

The relative importance accorded to the available sources of information varies with industry and with typology. Figure 3 shows key sources of information used to make strategic investment decisions in Ukraine.

First-Movers are largely dependent upon information generated via Ukrainian Joint Venture partners whereby they gain access to such information as exists. First-Movers were found exclusively in consumer product markets. The majority of information which they require relates to potential end consumers. Little secondary data is available. Hence, primary research has been carried out by internal market research staff and by local business schools.

Client-Followers are often initially dependent upon the network links

FIGURE 2. Major Influences on Strategic Investments in Ukraine

CLIENT FOLLOWERS

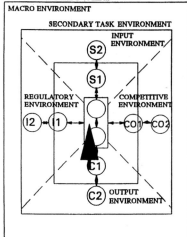

OPTION-TAKERS

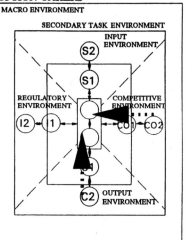

FIRST-MOVERS

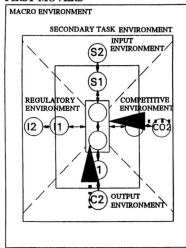

DEAL-MAKERS

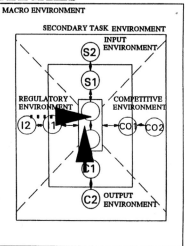

I = INTEREST GROUP
C = CUSTOMER

CO = COMPETITOR
S = SUPPLIER

Based on Figure 1 "Environment of Marketing Channel Dyads" Achrol, Reve and Stern *Journal of Marketing* 1983

FIGURE 3. Major Sources of Information Used to Make Strategic Investment Decisions in Ukraine

CLIENT FOLLOWERS
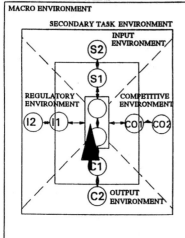

OPTION-TAKERS
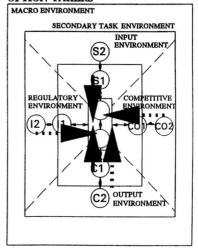

FIRST-MOVERS
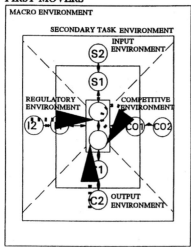

DEAL-MAKERS
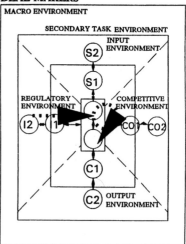

I = INTEREST GROUP   CO = COMPETITOR
C = CUSTOMER   S = SUPPLIER

Based on Figure 1 "Environment of Marketing Channel Dyads" Achrol, Reve and Stern *Journal of Marketing* 1983.

of their industrial customers in Ukraine. However, they also use their existing network relationships within the organization and in other markets.

Deal-Makers exchange flows of information with the government and external funding bodies who influence their decision to invest in Ukraine. Details of further funding opportunities are received via these links. Expert knowledge is given in return. These firms count themselves as a major source of reliable information in the market. They were cited by a number of option-takers as a major source of information.

Option-Takers, in accordance with their objective to assess the potential of the Ukrainian market, use all available sources of information. In industrial markets, government bodies responsible for the particular industry have some statistical information. Investment activity of key global customers is monitored, as are actions of oligopolistic rivals in the market.

8. THE PROCESS OF INVESTMENT

The pattern of entry into the Ukraine does not fit with Johanson and Vahlne's process model (1977). The different levels of investment may not be sequentially linked. Moreover, preliminary findings support the view that size of firm, length of international experience and distinction between product or service firms may influence the mode of investment. Moreover, the strategic goals of the firm in entering the market play a significant role.

Prior to the breakdown of the Soviet Union, a number of firms had already invested in facilities in geographic proximity to the Ukrainian market. These were in some cases used as a base to prospect the market. In one case, a Joint Venture agreement had been entered into, prior to the breakup of the Soviet Union. Despite the dramatically different environmental conditions, this proceeded as the identification of a "good" Joint Venture partner was seen to be a more important consideration than the changes in the environment.

The lowest level of investment in Ukraine is the representative office, which cannot trade. This requires only nominal levels of investment. Slightly higher investment is required for a wholly-owned subsidiary, which allows the firm to trade in Ukraine. The highest level of investment found in the cases studied is in the Manufacturing Joint Ventures. Percentage stakes held in Joint Ventures varies. Theoretically, acquisition of plants is possible, but a local partner tends to be preferred. Investment in greenfield manufacturing operations is hampered by current legislation on property ownership.

9. CONCLUSIONS

This preliminary analysis has identified differences between broad groups of strategic investment decisions. It has provided a better understanding of the variables which were considered relevant in entry and expansion decisions by Western firms in the Ukrainian context. A number of conclusions can be drawn. Firstly, that information does flow between stakeholders in the Ukrainian market. However, the flows may be partially linked to the previous system of government. It is not yet clear whether these will be replaced by exchange relationships more like those in Western markets.

Secondly, the groups of firms exhibit different views as to the level of commitment which is necessary to gain knowledge about the Ukraine. Deal-Makers and Client-Followers consider that sufficient information can be gained by the use of existing network relationships.

However, First-Movers and Option-Takers consider that integration into local networks is necessary. They differ as to the speed at which they are prepared to make the necessary commitment to do this. A reason for these different views may be the different requirements of serving industrial customers and consumer markets.

Finally, firms differ as to the level of risk which they take in entering Ukraine. First-Movers have accepted the high level of risk involved in commitment to the market as the "price" for the benefit of building defensible market-share. This is recognised as a long-term strategy. Option-Takers take a cautious approach which seems most in keeping with the process model. Both Client-Followers and Deal-Makers make high levels of commitment, but find ways of reducing the risk which this poses to the firm. Both build upon existing relationships in order to do this (see Figure 4).

However, the preliminary analysis raises a number of additional ques-

FIGURE 4

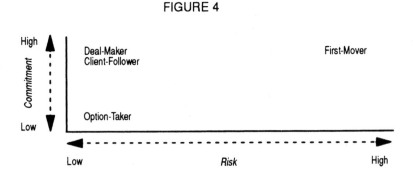

tions which require further research. Firstly, what level of commitment to the market–where commitment is not simply a financial investment, but the totality of factors which the firms has staked in entering its current form of operation–is necessary to operate effectively in the Ukraine? Is presence in the market in a low commitment mode sufficient to operate effectively, or should firms adopt the highest possible level of investment to gain maximum benefit. Secondly, can firms gain sufficient knowledge to operate effectively in Ukraine from existing network relationships? Thirdly, are firms who build on existing relationships in entering the market still influenced by these relationships in subsequent decisions which they make? What impact does this have on their performance? Finally, is the specific country in which the investment is made of relevance in the decision? Firms were often more concerned about the actions of oligopolistic rivals than about the specifics of the market situation. What further understanding of entry and expansion decisions do we gain if these decisions are seen as moves in a larger "game"?

10. LIMITATIONS

It is recognised that this paper raises many more questions than it can answer. However, this is in accordance with its exploratory nature. Many of the above questions require longitudinal study and revision of the research instrument.

BIBLIOGRAPHY

Achrol, R. S., Reve, T. and Stern, L. W. (1983). "The Environment of Marketing Channel Dyads: A Framework for Comparative Analysis." *Journal of Marketing*, pp. 55-67.

Buckley, P. J. (1991). "Developments in International Business Theory in the 1990s." *Journal of Marketing Management*, 7, pp. 15-24.

Clark, T. and Mallory, G. (1992). "The Stages Theory of Internationalisation: A Conceptual and Empirical Critique." Paper delivered to the British Academy of Management Conference, Bradford.

De Wit, A. and Monami, E. (1993). "Doing Business in an Unstable Environment: The Case of the Ex-USSR." Proceedings of the 9th IMP Conference, Bath 1993.

Dicthl, E., Leibold, M., Köglmayer, H. G. and Müller, S. (1984). "The Export Decision of Small and Medium-Sized Firms: A Review." *Journal of International Management*, 24, pp. 49-60.

Egan, C. E. (1993). "Theoretical Constraints on Marketing Practice: Challenging Orthodoxy." Proceedings of the Rethinking Marketing Symposium, Warwick.

Erramilli, K. (1990). "Entry Mode Choice in Service Industries." *International Marketing Review*, 7, 5.

Etgar, M. (1978). "Selection of an Effective Channel Control Mix." *Journal of Marketing Research* 15, July pp. 53-58.

Forsgren, M. (1989). *Managing the Internationalisation Process: The Swedish Case*. Routledge.

Håkansson, H. (1982). *International Marketing and Purchasing of Industrial Goods: An Interaction Approach*. Croom Helm.

Håkansson, H. and Johanson, J. (1992). "A Model of Industrial Networks" in Easton, G. and Axelsson, B. (eds.) *Industrial Networks: A New View of Reality*. Routledge.

Håkansson, H. and Wootz, B. (1975a). "Supplier Selection in an International Environment–An Experimental Study." *Journal of Marketing Research*.

Håkansson, H. and Wootz, B. (1975b). "Risk Reduction and the Industrial Purchaser." *European Journal of Marketing* 9, 1 pp. 35-51.

Harrigan, K. (1983). "Research Methodologies for Contingency Approaches to Business Strategy" in *Academy of Management Review*, 8(3), pp. 398-405.

Hickson, D. J., Butler, R. J., Cray, D., Mallory, G. R., and Wilson, D. C. (1985). *Top Decisions*. Blackwell.

Jatar, A. (1992). Unpublished PhD Dissertation, University of Warwick.

Johanson, J. and Mattsson, L. G. (1988). "Internationalization in Industrial Systems–A Network Approach" in N. Hood and J. Vahlne (ed.) *Strategies in Global Competition*. London: Croom Helm.

Johanson, J. and Sharma, D. (1987). "Technical Consultancy in Internationalization." *International Marketing Review*, 4, pp. 20-29.

Johanson, J. and Vahlne, J. E. (1977). "The Internationalisation Process of the Firm: A Model of Knowledge Development on Increasing Foreign Commitments." *Journal of International Business Studies*, Spring/Summer pp. 23-32.

Johanson, J. and Vahlne, J. E. (1990). "The Mechanism of Internationalisation." *International Marketing Review*, 7, 4 pp. 11-24.

Johanson, J. and Wiedersheim-Paul, F. (1975). "The Internationalisation of the Firm–Four Swedish Cases." *Journal of Management Studies*. 12, pp. 305-322.

Lusch, R. F. (1976). "Sources of Power: Their Impact on Intra-Channel Conflict." *Journal of Marketing Research*, 13, pp. 382-390.

Manninen, K. and Snelbecker, D. (1993). "Obstacles to Doing Business in Ukraine." Project on Economic Reform in Ukraine, Harvard University.

Miles, R. E. and Snow, C. C. (1986). "Organisations: New concepts for New Forms." *California Management Review*, 28, pp. 62-73.

Mattsson, L. G. (1993). "The Role of Marketing for the Transformation of a Centrally Planned Economy to a Market Economy." *Economics and Marketing: Essays in Honour of Gösta Mickwitz*. Swedish School of Economics and Business Administration, Finland.

Penrose, E. (1959). *The Theory of Growth of the Firm*. Blackwell, Oxford.

Porter, M. E. (1985). *Competitive Advantage*. Free Press.

Pyatt, R. (1993). "The Preliminary Model of the Soviet-Type Command Network: A Study of Industrial Networks in Vietnam's Liberalising Period." Proceedings of the 9th IMP Conference, Bath 1993.

Tesar, G. (1993). "Internationalisation of New and Privatised Firms in Transitionary Economics of Central and Eastern Europe: Phasing Out of the Old Contractual into New Voluntary Networks." Proceedings of the 9th IMP Conference, Bath 1993.

Thorelli, H. B. (1986). "Networks: Between Markets and Hierarchies." *Strategic Management Journal*, 7, pp. 37-51.

Turnbull, P. W. (1987). "A Challenge to the Stages Theory of the Internationalization Process" in P. J. Rosson and S. D. Reed (eds) *Managing Export Entry and Expansion*. New York: Praeger.

Turnbull, P. W. and Valla, J. P. (1986). *Strategies for International Industrial Marketing*. Routledge.

Young, L. C. and Wilkinson, I. F. (1989). "The Role of Trust and Co-Operation in Marketing Channels: A Preliminary Study." *European Journal of Marketing*, 23 pp. 109-122.

Williamson, O. E. (1975). *Markets and Hierarchies: Analysis and Antitrust Implications*. Macmillan.

Yin, R. (1989). *Case Study Research: Design and Methods*. Sage.

Western Strategies in Central Europe

Peter Haiss
Gerhard Fink

SUMMARY. This paper explores investment patterns of Western firms which became active in Eastern Europe since the fall of the Soviet Empire. Strategic market characteristics and resulting entry strategies are depicted. Contrary to general belief, the conclusion is drawn that weak, not strong, companies have invested, bearing severe implications for financiers. *[Article copies available from The Haworth Document Delivery Service: 1-800-342-9678.]*

INTRODUCTION

On the one hand, it is clear that the fall of the Soviet Empire opened up vast new opportunities for Western companies: access to roughly 400 million potential retail clients, equivalent to about 8% of the world's population. An infrastructure that needs to be rebuilt from scratch, with vast investment opportunities in production facilities. Another advantage is labor cost of about one tenth of Western European average, while at the

---

Peter R. Haiss is affiliated with Bank Austria, AM Hof 2, A-1010 Wien, Austria.

Gerhard Fink is affiliated with Wirtschaftsuniversität Wien, Althanstrasse 39-45, A-1090 Wien, Austria.

This paper was submitted for presentation at the workshop "Strategies for Entering Eastern European Markets" by Wirtschaftsuniversität Wien and DePaul University, Chicago, November 25 and 26, 1993, Vienna.

[Haworth co-indexing entry note]: "Western Strategies in Central Europe." Haiss, Peter, and Gerhard Fink. Co-published simultaneously in *Journal of East-West Business* (International Business Press, an imprint of The Haworth Press, Inc.) Vol. 1, No. 3, 1995, pp. 37-45; and: *The Central and Eastern European Markets: Guideline for New Business Ventures* (ed: Petr Chadraba) International Business Press, an imprint of The Haworth Press, Inc., 1995, pp. 37-45. Single or multiple copies of this article are available from The Haworth Document Delivery Service [1-800-342-9678, 9:00 a.m. - 5:00 p.m. (EST)].

same time major parts of the total labor force are highly skilled. There certainly are numerous drawbacks and risks involved, ranging from environmental pollution, ownership problems, and political uncertainty to the lack of financial markets. A great challenge for well-suited Western companies to enter these markets, one might think. Well, there exist already around 50,000 joint ventures with Western participation in former Eastern Europe, with total direct investment of Western companies of about 14 billion US dollars.

Thus, it is worthwhile to explore investment patterns of Western firms which became active in Eastern Europe since the fall of the Soviet Empire. Differences in market structures to Western markets are explained, using financial markets as an example. Resulting implications for investors and their respective entry strategies are depicted. Contrary to general belief, the conclusion is drawn that weak, not strong, companies have invested, bearing severe implications for financiers: while Eastern companies at sale are usually of high substance value, they are also of low profitability.

DISCONTINUITY AS OPPORTUNITY

Eastern Europe is an area that has sought to integrate itself again into the world economy in recent years. That shift from centrally-planned, autarky-driven economies which were sheltered from world competition into open, market-oriented economies can be classified as strategic shock, resulting in total discontinuity of market forces. This has both positive and negative implications for the respective economies and companies active in these markets. Major positive signs of reconstructing the economies can be found in the development of private sector companies. The partial economic paralysis of the state-owned sector is set off against the steadily growing private and semi-private sector. According to estimates based on the market value of companies (Haiss, 1992), the private sector in Hungary and Poland already accounts for roughly 20-30% of the total economy, around 10% in Czechoslovakia, but less in the other countries of the former Council of Mutual Economic Assistance (CMEA). Also, a fast growth of foreign direct investment leads to the conclusion that investors have a positive view about economic prospects for several countries. The number of joint ventures with Western capital located in CMEA countries rose from 514 (1983) to 3,400 (1990) and exploded to roughly 50,000 till the end of 1992 (Debs et al., 1991; Andreff, 1991; Stankovsky, 1992). Impulses for structural change now originate above all in foreign trade. In 1990, for example, Western European exports to Eastern Europe rose by 2.4% in real terms to a total of $bn 64.5 (Gabrisch, 1992).

However, these countries in transition also encounter many problems (Williamson, 1991; IMF, 1992). In Russia, Bulgaria, and Romania, industrial production has been falling by roughly 15-25% a year since 1989, and 5-10% for the Central European countries. In 1991 gross domestic product standards (GDP), the Visegrad countries of Poland, Hungary, and the Czech and Slovak Republics reached not even 10% of the U.S. GDP per capita. It is obvious that economic structures in Eastern European countries are seriously distorted, giving rise to the wastage of economic resources on a massive scale (Brainard, 1992). The structural problems that surfaced in the centrally planned countries are a direct outcome of several anomalies inherent in the previous system. Western companies investing in these markets still have to tackle these problems. For example, a regular financial system viable to every economy was virtually suppressed and non-existent.

INVESTMENT AND THE LACK OF FINANCIAL MARKETS

In Hungary, Poland and the Czech and Slovak Republics, as well as in every other place, the size of a financial market depends on the economic strength of a country (GDP per capita), its size (total GDP), and institutional issues. However, due to continued macroeconomic problems of banking in the past, financial markets in the Visegrad countries are very small. For example, total financial intermediation in Hungary, Czechoslovakia and Poland currently is at a level of about one tenth of Austria and even one twentieth of Switzerland, countries otherwise comparable in size. Financial markets in Eastern Europe are even smaller than total assets of Bank Austria, which is one of the most active Western banks in Central Europe, with total assets of roughly $bn 50 (1991) (see Table 1).[1]

Poland's financial market matches 70% of Bank Austria ($bn 37.4), the Czech and Slovak financial markets together about 60% ($bn 29.3), and Hungary about 50% ($bn 23.7). Stock market capitalization (1991) was at $bn 0.5 in Hungary, $bn 1.4 in Poland, against $bn 22.2 in Austria. In an international comparison, sight deposits (H: $bn 3.4, PL: $bn 6.1, CSFR: $bn 10.2) are more important than in the Western world (e.g., Austria: $bn 14.3; all data 1991). For term deposits, we can observe the opposite: H $bn 8.0, CSFR $bn 11.7, PL $bn 13.9 against Austria at $bn 137.1. The connection with international financial markets through foreign assets and liabilities is also comparatively low, although the international debt burden is still there as an overhang. Thus, there are still various leftover structural differences between financial systems in Eastern Europe and Western standards that are of influence to Western companies' investment decisions (Brainard, 1992; Handler et al., 1992; Zwass, 1986):

TABLE 1. European Financial Markets Total Financial Intermediation (1991 data in billion US-$)

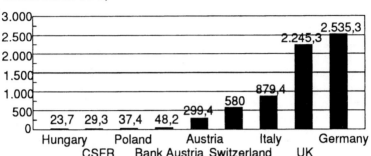

- *National banks' relative importance:* National banks play a larger role in the overall market in terms of business volume. In Hungary, about a quarter of the total financial market volume are banks' deposits and credits with the Hungarian National Bank. In Poland, about a fifth of total bank credits are credits against the national bank.
- *Large foreign exchange risks:* In Hungary, 85% of total savings deposits, 30% of corporate deposits with banks, and 57% of banks' deposits with the national bank are held in foreign currency.
- *Cumulative devaluation losses:* About a third of the total assets of the Hungarian National Bank, as well as 15% of total assets of Polish banks are accumulated devaluation losses.
- *Large sour credits:* 1991 estimates by the Hungarian National Bank account for 716 illiquid companies with FTbn 160 in liable credits, including FTbn 88 in writeoffs and FTbil 8 in provisions. By April 1992, additional 2,000 companies were announced to be in bankruptcy, 3,200 under liquidation. In the combined Czech and Slovak Republics, over 20% of total financial market volume (over KCSbn 170) are endangered or irrevocable.

ADDITIONAL RISKS OF INVESTING IN EASTERN EUROPE

Besides the general economic risks described in the introductory section, and the risks resulting from the shaky financial system in Eastern European countries, Western companies have to be aware of additional risk triggers:
- *The Western owner:* There is often a lack of free strategic capacity, i.e., the "Eastern" jobs come on top of the already existing tasks.

Unfamiliarity with local conditions as well as communication and distance barriers often are unprecedented problems for controlling and supervising local management. In the East, the capacity for raising additional capital is also often overestimated.

- *Management:* Western managers are often under severe strain due to frequent communication problems. Language and cultural differences heavily draw on the conflict potential of Western managers. Eastern managers, while suffering from the same communication problems are, in addition, often short-term oriented. Either because they lack the know-how for long-term strategies, or because their work pattern is just oriented towards short-term survival.
- *Personnel:* Similar to managers. Very often workers need a boss who is both a coach (listens), trainer (designs the operative strategy) and motivator (creates commitment). Especially frightening to westerners are the problems of fighting non-involvement and non-commitment. Workers are ridden by severe problems in their daily life (insufficient housing, varying consumer supplies and the like) which have a rather strong effect on their motivation.
- *Environment:* Suppliers often are unreliable, there may also be a lack of distribution channels. Clients' credibility very often is at risk and beyond the supplier's control due to the lack of company records and reliable bank inquiries. Local banks often are of doubtful credibility themselves, and payment systems can be described as slow at best. Local capital is scarce and, if available, either black money or tied into credits for inefficient state-run companies.

STRATEGIC PATTERNS OF WESTERN COMPANIES IN EASTERN EUROPE

From the data presented above, popular arguments for luring investment to Eastern Europe could be drawn (Richter and Stankovsky, 1991): low labor costs, a large undersupplied market of 400 million people, large growth potential, and a variety of vast natural resources (Poland, Russia, Ukraine, Kazakhstan). Given the high uncertainty about market development in the East, the risk of entering Eastern Europe, however, is mostly taken by Western firms which apparently have little to lose. Western companies to a large extent become active in Eastern Europe not because they are the strongest companies in their respective markets, building on their strengths abroad, but because they use Eastern Europe as a resort of last hope. In the case of small- and medium-sized companies, they are very often undercapitalised. In the case of large companies, they are very often structurally weak. Companies' real motives for investment, therefore, are rather weak local competition, low cost of labor, and the drive for global presence of powerful brands. Weak local competition lures foreign companies with low capital ratios. Low-cost labor lures companies which are themselves ridden by structural problems in their home countries. Thus, there is a disparity between what is usually quoted as a reason for Western activities and the actual motives.

Transnational corporations, for example, are engaged as much as they are obliged to secure global presence for global brand names. They go for joint ventures to test the water at best. These joint ventures, however, often are merely sales or service units. Production units are set up rather rarely, and if so, only with selected partners. They regard the investment as a part of a world-wide marketing and sales concept, bringing Western products into Eastern distribution channels. Heavy capital investments are possible, but follow a lengthy real-world examination of possible partners (cooperation, outsourcing, etc.). Typical examples are soft drink companies like Coca-Cola™ and Pepsi-Cola™, or brand-exploiting companies like McDonalds'™ restaurants as well as technology-companies as Siemens.

Small- and medium-sized companies with good management potential often rather eye Western than Eastern markets. However, those with structural problems often try to play the role of being the stronger among the weak in the East, rather than trying to beat equals in the West. Three patterns emerge (see Table 2):

- *The gold-rush companies:* Many such companies want to make quick money. They hope for fast expansion, bet on the new markets, while themselves being backed by heavy debt burdens. They crumble due to low management-capacity, undercapitalization and resulting high cost of capital, the unavailability of venture capital for Eastern Europe, and payment risk and resulting liquidity shortages. A significant number of newly founded trading companies are typically falling under this category.
- *Companies targeting Western clients:* Many companies invest in East-Central Europe not to conquer the local market, but to keep or retain Western clients. This pattern is shown by industries with low-mobility production, a large fraction of capital expenditures and low fraction of personnel expenditure in total costs, and weak local competition. Hotels are typically falling under this category. They are financed by bank loans, backed by national and semi-national export guarantee institutions or mortgage loans where possible.
- *Companies cutting cost for Western clients:* Cost-driven companies often show a strong mobility of production, low capital cost and large labor-cost shares and seek weak local competition. The textile

and textile-related industries are quite typical for such moves. They are often financed by trade finance and leasing arrangements as well as through buy-backs and other forms of barter arrangements handled by trade finance companies.

Large companies, similar to their smaller counterparts, try to use the newly opened markets as an escape from unresolved problems in their respective home markets or company-internal structures. Two different patterns can be observed (Abbell, 1991; Schremmer and Krajasits, 1992):

- *Defensive strategy:* Western companies in highly regulated and thereby protected markets, with inherent low mobility of production try to keep competition at arm's length through Eastern European investments. Their company size makes it possible to raise money in the domestic capital markets. Steel, paper, food, cement, car und brewery companies are typical examples.
- *Wunderwaffen strategy:* Companies facing illiquidity, bankruptcy or closure in their respective home markets promise wunderwaffen-like superinvestments in the opening markets frequently based on public support (that is, if their respective governments subsidize them) in order to "remain" competitive. In that way the reform countries are competing with Greece, Portugal, Ireland, Spain and others, exploiting comparative advantages for luring business into their respective region.

CONCLUSION

While there are many signs of positive development in Eastern Europe, one must not accept the argument that the many Western companies active in Eastern Europe will necessarily give a boost to these markets and economies. As many of these companies rather try to overcome their own weaknesses by entering Eastern European markets instead of building on their strengths, their trigger effect on the respective economies will be limited and may even turn out to be to the detriment of a development towards market economies. There are several implications that can be drawn from this observation. Firstly, banks need to be very cautious in providing finance for Western joint ventures. Secondly, Eastern European companies also need to explore the relative standing and situation of Western companies that try to lure them into joint ventures. Thirdly, Eastern European governments, as well as the two groups just mentioned, need to engage in strategic strength/weakness analysis of Western companies in attracting the right investment. Fourth, as rebuilding Eastern Europe takes longer than initially thought, many weak Western companies will quickly pull out again.

TABLE 2. Real Western Strategies

	Defensive	Test-the-Water	Wunderwaffen
	to keep competition at arm's length	Low-key investment to at least have tried it	to overcome failure by obtaining "fresh" subsidies
	West-Targets	Cost-Cutting	Gold-Rush
	no interest in Eastern markets, but following Western clients	move production unit only	highly leveraged to make a quick buck

Size ↑

Degree of Despair in Home Market →

NOTE

1. Bank Austria is Austria's largest universal bank and was chosen as a referent because it is one of the most active Western banks in Central Europe. In the U.S., First Chicago Corp. is of about the same size in terms of total assets, equivalent to rank 13 in terms of total equity among U.S. banks (Blanden/Timewell, 1992).

REFERENCES

Abell, D. 1991. Closing the Management Gap in Eastern Europe. In Haskins, K. & Purg, D., *Developing Managers for Eastern and Central Europe*. Brussels, B: European Foundation for Management Development.
Andreff, W. 1991. Soviet Foreign Trade Reforms and the Challenge to East European Economic Relations with the West. In Bertsch, G. & Elliott-Gower, S. (eds.), *The Impact of Governments on East-West Economic Relations*, 14:23-46. London, UK: MacMillan.
Blanden, M. & Timewell, S. 1991. Top 1000 Banks. *Banker*, 66 (7):66-167.
Brainard, L. 1991. Eastern Europe: Creating a Capital Market. *The AMEX Bank Review Prize Essays*, 4:1-22. Oxford, UK: Oxford University Press.
Debs, R., Shapiro, H., & Taylor, C. 1991. *Financing Eastern Europe*. Washington, DC: Group of Thirty.
Gabrisch, H. 1992. Advanced Reforming Countries Might Reach End of Recession. *WIIW Forschungsberichte*, 184:1-14.
Haiss, P. 1992. Notwendige Randbedingungen für die Reformen in Osteuropa. *Wirtschaftspolitische Blätter*, 39 (1).
Haiss, P. Central European Strategies of Austrian Banks. *Bankarchiv*, 39 (5):327-335.
Handler, H., Kramer, H., & Stankovsky, J. 1992. *Debt, Capital Requirement and Financing of the Eastern Countries*. Vienna, A: Austrian Institute of Economic Research.
Richter, S., & Stankovsky, J. 1991. *Die neue Rolle Österreichs im Ost-West-Handel*. Vienna, A: Vienna Institute for Comparative Economic Studies.
IMF, 1992. *World Economic Outlook October 1992*. Washington, DC: International Monetary Fund.
Schremmer, C. & C. Krajasits. 1992. Szenarien zur Ost-Grenzöffnung und deren Auswirkungen auf die öster-reichischen Ost-Grenzregionen. *Schriften zur Regional-politik und Raumplanung*, 20.
Stankovsky, J. 1992. Die Oststaaten und ihre Banken. *Internationale Wirtschaft*, 36 (9):15.
Williamson, D. *The Economic Opening of Eastern Europe*. Washington, DC: Institute for International Economics.
Zwass, A. 1986. *Money, Banking and Credit in the Soviet Union and Eastern Europe*. London, UK: MacMillan.

Potential Market Opportunities in Hungary, Poland and Bulgaria

Tony Cox

Graham Hooley

SUMMARY. Central European economies are undergoing radical reforms changing from central planning to free market economies. If these changes are to be successful, there is a need for their governments to liberalise legislation to allow privatisation to take place and to allow and encourage foreign investment in the countries. Potentially the most effective form of foreign investment is the participation of Western companies in the business of the country enabling development of the market and the local understanding of the methods of business in free market economies. Whether and to what extent this participation takes place depends on the macro-environmental climate and the specific market environments in the countries. This paper addresses both of these issues and is based on a twelve month study of marketing conditions in Hungary, Poland and Bulgaria.

In the first part the macro changes taking place are explored and the overall attractiveness assessed by comparison with the published literature on the market entry strategies. The conclusion is that Hungary is the most attractive of the three countries concerned for Western company investment in terms of political stability, economic development and performance, cultural unity, and lower legal and geo-cultural similarity.

Tony Cox and Graham Hooley are affiliated with Aston Business School, Aston University, The Triangle, Birmingham, B4 7ET, England.

[Haworth co-indexing entry note]: "Potential Market Opportunities in Hungary, Poland and Bulgaria." Cox, Tony, and Graham Hooley. Co-published simultaneously in *Journal of East-West Business* (International Business Press, an imprint of The Haworth Press, Inc.) Vol. 1, No. 3, 1995, pp. 47-66; and: *The Central and Eastern Eurpopean Markets: Guideline for New Business Ventures* (ed: Petr Chadraba) International Business Press, an imprint of The Haworth Press, Inc., 1995, pp. 47-66. Single or multiple copies of this article are available from The Haworth Document Delivery Service [1-800-342-9678, 9:00 a.m. - 5:00 p.m. (EST)].

47

The second part of the paper explores the changing market environments specific to each country and is based on 2100 responses to a questionnaire sent to the chief marketing executives of companies. The field work was carried out by local nationals in the countries concerned enabling the normal marketing concepts to be put in the national context. The impact of the changes in the local market environment was further explored by identifying both the key factors necessary for success in each country and where local companies have competitive advantage or disadvantage. In this way opportunities for Western company involvement are identified. Focus on these issues will allow both the country and the investing company to benefit.

The main findings are that, overall, the provision of improved product quality, reliability and range at competitive and affordable prices is essential. The input of Western technological, distribution and marketing experience would be especially beneficial. Specific country requirements are the need for more customer choice and cost reduction in Hungary; in Poland the same criteria apply with the addition of an increased response to customer requirements; in Bulgaria the provision of effective distribution channels is of paramount importance.

Despite the obvious risks in investing in these countries there are considerable opportunities that represent a chance of developing the countries and providing an investment opportunity for Western companies. *[Article copies available from The Haworth Document Delivery Service: 1-800-342-9678.]*

1. INTRODUCTION

Central European countries are in the process of transition from centrally planned to market-led economies. The transition process has been in progress for different lengths of time, implemented in different ways by each country, and met with varying levels of success. The rate at which they progress depends not only on the economic and political environment, but also on the help that they receive from the West. This help can take many forms but a potentially important investment is for Western companies to participate in their business and trade. This can be expected to modernise their production processes, develop their distribution channels, and help in their learning process. The objectives of any Western involvement should therefore be twofold: firstly to help in the progress to fully operational free market economies, and secondly to obtain a reasonable return for this investment (Mann 1991).

This paper investigates the theoretical and practical aspects of potential Western involvement and identifies some potential opportunities. It is based on the results of a twelve month comparative study of marketing environments, attitudes, organisation and strategies in the three Central European countries of Hungary, Poland and Bulgaria.

2. ECONOMIC BACKGROUND

The progress towards a free economy depends on many factors including the state of the economy, the effect that the changes have on the living standards of the population and the understanding and application of marketing activities. The issues are inextricably linked and need to be mutually supportive. If the economy is not strong then marketing opportunities may be difficult to exploit because of lack of investment. If the living standards of the population decrease this may reduce political commitment to further progress. The situation is very different in each of the three countries. These macro-environmental differences are outlined in the rest of this section based on data from the *CIA World Fact Book* (1992).

2.1 Hungary

Hungary's economic reform programmes, which started during the Communist era, gave it a head start in creating a free market economy and attracting foreign investment. In 1990 it received half of all foreign investment in Central Europe and in 1991 received the largest single share. Privatisation of state enterprises is progressing but is hampered by excessive red tape and uncertainties about pricing. The private sector accounts for a quarter to a third of the national output. Industry accounts for about 40% of the GDP and 30% of the employment. Less than 20% of foreign trade is now with the former COMECON countries, while about 70% is with the OECD. Escalating unemployment and high rates of inflation are impeding efforts to speed up privatisation and budget reforms, while its heavy foreign debt will make the government reluctant to introduce full convertibility of its currency.

2.2 Poland

In 1990 the government implemented shock treatment by dramatically reducing subsidies, decontrolling prices, tightening the money supply, stabilising the foreign exchange rate, lowering import barriers, and restraining state sector wages. This resulted in consumer goods shortages but caused inflation to fall from 640% in 1989 to 60% in 1991. At the same time Western governments, which hold two-thirds of Poland's $48 billion external debt, pledged to forgive half of this debt by 1994. As a result the private sector grew and accounted for 22% of industrial production and 40% of non-agricultural output by 1991. State enterprise production fell despite this and the unemployment rate increased to 11.4% in 1992. This has led to popular discontent and to two changes of government in 1991 and 1992. The new government has promised selective industrial intervention, relaxation in monetary policy, and improved social safety net. This is both constrained by and constrains the growing budget deficit. Despite this the Polish economy has shown considerable growth in the first half of 1993 as reported in *The Economist* of September 1993, however, the results of the recent elections could well retard the process.

2.3 Bulgaria

In 1990, Bulgaria's foreign debt was over $10 billion, which gave a debt-service ratio of more than 40% of its hard currency earnings. The post-Communist government is facing major problems of replacing ageing industrial plants, coping with worsening energy, food and consumer goods shortages, and keeping abreast of technological innovation. A major problem is the motivation of the population, which it is doing by giving them a share in the earnings of their enterprises. The government is strongly committed to economic reform and has eased restrictions on foreign investment and liberalised currency trading. Very little privatisation has taken place although small entrepreneurs are emerging and the government has passed bills to privatise large state-owned enterprises. It is interesting that negotiations have started on an association of agreement with the EC.

The implications of these differences between the countries are discussed below.

3. GENERAL THEORETICAL CONTEXT

It has been argued above that Western participation, in terms of investment, trade and training, has an important part to play in the free market development of the Central European countries. The environment of the country concerned will determine, to a large degree, whether and to what extent this will happen. The investing company will try to reduce its risks and indeed the decision process is one of risk reduction. The potential rewards are, however, considerable. Together, Eastern Europe and the USSR represent a major untapped market. It is a market of more than 420 million people but there is uncertainty about the potential outcome of the reform programmes and austerity measures under way (Siren and Shaw 1991).

Goodnow and Hansz (1972) indicate that companies will tend to participate more fully in a country if its environment is perceived to be favourable. In their work favourable countries are defined as those having high levels of political stability, market opportunity, economic development and performance, cultural unity, low legal and physiographic barriers and geocultural distance. They place countries on a spectrum between favourable (hot) and unfavourable (cold). For countries in the favourable category, companies tend to undertake a greater involvement with full foreign manufacturing and distribution often using Joint Ventures for this purpose. For countries at the other end of the spectrum investing companies tend to reduce their risks by using direct exporting and local agents and distributors.

Goodnow (1985), in a separate study, found that the amount of investment in the manufacturing and distribution channels is considerably affected by the environment of the country. From the previous sections, Hungary represents less of a risk than Bulgaria and it is entirely consistent that it has attracted the bulk of foreign investment while Bulgaria has attracted relatively little. Other factors can alter the foreign perception of risk. Among these, one of the most important is the amount of government stimulation given in terms of legal and economic help. Already, new laws in Poland, and Hungary have promoted joint ventures that allow for any equity agreed between the partners (Boudette 1989), while the Bulgarian government seems to have recognised this in the political and economic moves noted above which should go some way to stimulating Western company participation.

Two key reforms underpin the moves toward more market-orientated economies in East-Central Europe: (1) Price reforms that allow a freer alignment of relative prices toward international norms and (2) industry reforms that increase competition, flexibility and efficiency (Mann 1991). Again, Hungary is seen to be in the most favourable position but Poland is making rapid progress in this respect.

Full participation is also influenced by geographic and cultural differences. In general terms full participation is more likely the more similar the target country is to that of the investing company (Anderson and Coughlan (1987), Klein and Roth (1990)). In the case of investment into Central Europe the investing company needs relevant expertise and resources. Again, Hungary is in a potentially better position than Bulgaria with Poland occupying an intermediate position.

Although these macro-environmental factors have a large influence on the propensity of companies to invest in Central European markets, other factors also play a considerable role. Some of these represent long term strategic goals, e.g., the Baltic states are positioned to be the staging area and main points of entry to the East (Locher 1992) as well as the local industrial conditions and indigenous technical capabilities. These can provide more specific opportunities even in apparently unfavourable countries. In order to exploit these there is need for a more detailed study of particular country situations. Weiner (1990) found that Western companies' knowledge of Central European markets, laws and customs is sometimes rudimentary. Williams (1993) noted that solid opportunities still exist for Western companies to enter the Eastern Europe market, but the organisations must temper their expectations for quick profits and invest more time in understanding local market culture. These specific market factors are investigated in the following sections of this paper.

4. METHODOLOGY

The methodology adopted consisted of qualitative and quantitative phases. In the qualitative phase, between 30 and 45 marketing managers were interviewed in each country to determine the format and detail of the questionnaire used in the quantitative phase. The sampling frame was constructed using the Standard Industry Classification and was representative of industry category, ownership, and company size. In each country 3000 companies were targeted in 3 waves. In Bulgaria, mailed questionnaires were used in the first two waves, producing a response of only 264. In the third wave, personally administered questionnaires were used for 1080 companies, resulting in a further 259 responses producing an overall response of 523. In all 2311 responses were received, 894 from both Hungary and Poland, and 523 from Bulgaria. The responses were checked for response wave bias using cross tabulations of the responses against the wave number. There were found to be no significant differences between the responses from different waves at the 0.001 confidence level. The results were analysed using the SPSSX statistical analysis package.

5. RESULTS

5.1 The Changing Marketing Environment

Respondents were asked to indicate whether they agreed, had no opinion or disagreed with a series of statements about the marketing environment in their country. They were also asked to comment on the likely impact using a three point scale from important, through no opinion, to unimportant. The issues covered by these statements had been elicited in the first phase of the research during the preliminary interviews. The findings are shown in Table 1, which gives the results for the overall sample together with the responses from each of the three countries. For each issue the significance of any difference is shown together with the chi squared value.

Overall the most frequently quoted factors were that customers will increasingly demand better quality and reliability (96% agreement), domestic and international competition will increase (86% and 77% agreement respectively), that customers would demand increasing choice (83% agreement), and that there would be an increased pressure on costs (82% agreement). These high priority factors are consistent with the likely changes caused by the move to free market economies with the concomitant increase in competition where superior quality, reliability and product choice can give a competitive edge. These issues would also provide an opportunity for foreign competitors to offer these benefits from a more efficient, lower cost base. The increased variety of goods providing for different customer needs will also encourage the emergence of new market segments whose particular needs match the different product characteristics. This was supported by 66% of respondents indicating that there would be an increase in the number of new emerging segments and that there would be an increase in the need for the customisation of both products and services.

Given that the progress towards free market economies involves the break-up of large state monopolies and the emergence of smaller more entrepreneurial companies the expected increase in the power of the distributors and retailers (60% agreement) is not unexpected. This again is an opportunity for Western investment to develop the distribution channels which are recognised to be fairly rudimentary in most Central European countries. On the other hand it is a source of difficulty for those companies who wish to enter these markets by marketing their goods through local distribution channels. There was fairly strong agreement that there would be more rapid technological change (53% agreement) and that this would lead to the reduction in product life cycles (42% agreement) and the shortening of lead times to market for new products (65% agreement). This, again, could represent an opportunity for Western companies to exploit their greater experience in this respect. Only a minority (39%) felt that there would be an increase in the movement towards standardisation and global products.

The importance of these factors follows almost exactly the ranking

TABLE 1. The Changing Marketing Environment

FACTOR		AGREEMENT			IMPACT		
		Agree	No Opinion	Disagree	Big	Some	None
Customers will increasingly demand better quality and reliability	Total n = 2183	95.7%	2.0%	2.3%	66.0%	30.5%	3.5%
	Hungary n = 823	95.4%	1.3%	3.3%	58.9%	36.7%	4.4%
	Poland n = 842	95.2%	2.1%	2.6%	60.3%	34.9%	4.8%
CHI SQUARE = 17.90 SIG = 0.001	Bulgaria n = 518	96.9%	2.9%	0.2%	82.4%	17.0%	0.6%
Domestic competition will increase	Total n = 2138	86.4%	7.1%	6.5%	58.5%	34.2%	7.3%
	Hungary n = 805	92.5%	2.6%	4.8%	64.1%	29.1%	6.8%
	Poland n = 810	81.4%	7.2%	11.5%	52.7%	37.4%	10.0%
CHI SQUARE = 121.25 SIG = 0.001	Bulgaria n = 523	84.9%	14.0%	1.1%	60.6%	35.4%	4.0%
International competition will increase	Total n = 2033	77.2%	17.4%	5.4%	47.2%	35.9%	16.9%
	Hungary n = 760	86.2%	11.3%	2.5%	44.1%	37.3%	18.6%
	Poland n = 750	73.9%	15.9%	10.3%	49.2%	28.8%	22.0%
CHI SQUARE = 119.69 SIG = 0.001	Bulgaria n = 523	68.8%	28.5%	2.7%	48.0%	44.0%	8.0%

	Agree	No Opinion	Disagree	Big	Some	None
Emergence of different customer segments with different needs and expectations						
Total n = 1948	66.1%	29.1%	4.9%	29.1%	50.9%	20.0%
Hungary n = 702	67.1%	27.5%	5.4%	26.9%	53.7%	19.4%
Poland n = 723	66.4%	26.6%	7.1%	24.5%	49.4%	26.1%
Bulgaria n = 523	64.2%	34.6%	1.1%	37.5%	49.7%	12.8%
CHI SQUARE = 30.44 SIG = 0.001						
Increasing customer choice						
Total n = 2100	82.5%	11.8%	5.7%	48.6%	40.8%	10.6%
Hungary n = 785	90.4%	3.4%	6.1%	50.5%	40.7%	8.8%
Poland n = 792	88.9%	4.8%	6.3%	55.5%	34.7%	9.9%
Bulgaria n = 523	61.0%	34.8%	4.2%	36.5%	49.7%	13.8%
CHI SQUARE = 356.90 SIG = 0.001						
Increasing customisation of products/services						
Total n = 2012	69.9%	17.5%	12.6%	43.7%	38.2%	18.2%
Hungary n = 737	64.9%	10.7%	24.4%	31.4%	42.4%	26.2%
Poland n = 752	85.0%	9.7%	5.3%	58.7%	31.7%	9.6%
Bulgaria n = 523	55.4%	38.2%	6.3%	36.9%	42.3%	20.8%
CHI SQUARE = 346.89 SIG = 0.001						

TABLE 1 (continued)

FACTOR		AGREEMENT			IMPACT		
		Agree	No Opinion	Disagree	Big	Some	None
Increased pressure on costs	Total n = 2122	81.6%	12.7%	5.7%	54.9%	35.1%	10.0%
	Hungary n = 801	92.9%	2.7%	4.4%	67.6%	28.6%	3.8%
CHI SQUARE = 335.02 SIG = 0.001	Poland n = 798	83.8%	8.0%	8.1%	58.4%	31.9%	9.8%
	Bulgaria n = 523	61.0%	35.0%	4.0%	35.9%	46.8%	17.2%
More rapid technological change	Total n = 1957	52.8%	29.3%	17.9%	29.7%	42.4%	27.9%
	Hungary n = 731	71.0%	16.1%	12.9%	32.5%	49.5%	18.0%
CHI SQUARE = 316.94 SIG = 0.001	Poland n = 703	31.4%	36.1%	32.4%	20.4%	37.8%	41.8%
	Bulgaria n = 523	56.0%	38.6%	5.4%	37.9%	40.0%	22.2%
Shorter lead times to market for new products	Total n = 1990	64.6%	27.0%	8.4%	35.4%	45.2%	19.4%
	Hungary n = 744	74.9%	14.4%	10.8%	34.6%	46.6%	18.8%
CHI SQUARE = 154.28 SIG = 0.001	Poland n = 723	65.3%	26.6%	8.2%	41.3%	35.1%	23.6%
	Bulgaria n = 523	48.9%	45.7%	5.4%	28.9%	56.4%	14.7%

		Agree	No Opinion	Disagree	Big	Some	None
Shorter life cycles for products	Total n = 1954	42.3%	35.4%	22.3%	22.5%	40.4%	37.1%
	Hungary n = 751	54.2%	19.4%	26.4%	21.1%	44.7%	34.2%
	Poland n = 680	31.8%	38.8%	29.4%	19.8%	31.6%	48.5%
CHI SQUARE = 224.26 SIG = 0.001	Bulgaria n = 523	39.0%	53.7%	7.3%	27.0%	46.1%	27.0%
Increasing standardisation towards global products	Total n = 1916	38.9%	44.5%	16.6%	18.4%	42.0%	39.6%
	Hungary n = 727	43.6%	35.9%	20.5%	13.0%	38.0%	49.1%
	Poland n = 666	26.3%	55.6%	18.2%	16.6%	33.5%	49.9%
CHI SQUARE = 98.52 SIG = 0.001	Bulgaria n = 523	48.4%	42.3%	9.4%	25.8%	55.6%	18.5%
Increasing power of retailers/distributors	Total n = 1974	60.0%	28.4%	11.7%	35.6%	37.7%	26.7%
	Hungary n = 745	73.8%	16.0%	10.2%	39.6%	36.3%	24.0%
	Poland n = 706	56.5%	29.2%	14.3%	38.7%	31.9%	29.4%
CHI SQUARE = 142.71 SIG = 0.001	Bulgaria n = 523	44.9%	44.9%	10.1%	27.5%	46.3%	26.2%

indicated above. In most cases the importance ranking and the frequency ranking are either the same or different by only one place. The two exceptions to this are the emergence of different customer segments which is seventh in the frequency ranking but tenth only in the importance ranking. A possible implication of this is that although new segments are likely to occur the local companies are unlikely to alter their method of doing business because of this. This may well be an opportunity for foreign traders. The second exception concerns the increasing power of distributors and retailers. This was ninth in the frequency ranking but seventh in the importance ranking. This is possibly a recognition of the deficiencies in the local distribution channels and supports the proposition that improved distribution is an important key to success in Central European markets.

5.1.1 Differences in the Marketing Environments of the Three Countries

One of the most obvious differences between the countries is the large percentage of Bulgarian respondents that expressed no opinion. This could well be a result of the smaller amount of progress made towards a free market economy and the consequent inability to appreciate the significance of the issues after only experiencing centrally planned economies for so long. This lack of marketing sophistication is noted in the work of Hooley et al. (1993).

Table 1 shows a high degree of agreement between the countries on the likely increase in demand for better quality and reliability, the increase in domestic competition, and the emergence of new segments. There is, however, less agreement on the likely impact of these factors. The increased demand for better quality and reliability is seen as having a greater impact in Bulgaria as does the emergence of new market segments. This could well represent the present poor base from which they are only now emerging. It is in Poland where the impact of increased domestic and international competition will have the least impact. This may well be the result of a product orientated philosophy of marketing (Hooley et al. 1993).

The Hungarian Marketing Environment

International competition is most likely to increase in Hungary but significantly is expected to have the least impact, possibly because this market is already exposed to foreign trade to a larger extent than the other two countries and has already come to terms with it. Increasing customer choice is seen as being the most likely and with the largest impact. There is also high importance attached to cost reduction, technological change, shorter product life cycles, and shorter lead times to market. In all of these areas Western companies are likely to have a competitive edge and, given the advantageous macro-environmental position of Hungary, this represents a good opportunity. This is also true of the increased power of distributors and retailers and is expected to have the most impact, reflecting the large expected progress of privatisation.

The Polish Marketing Environment

Despite the expected increase in domestic competition this is expected to have the least impact of the three countries. It would seem that the expected increase in the customisation of products and services will provide extra outlets and reduce the impact of increased competition. It is surprising that rapid technological change, reduced product life cycles, and decreased lead times in Poland are seen to have the least importance of the three countries. It may be that this is an area they feel they cannot develop and perhaps is a fruitful area for Western intervention.

The Bulgarian Marketing Environment

Bulgarian respondents indicate that the demand for better quality and reliability will have the greatest impact of all three countries possibly reflecting the lack of these two at present. This might well be an opportunity for Western companies to enter the market and to help their Bulgarian colleagues to achieve this required quality. International competition is expected to have the least impact of the three countries which is consistent with the macro selection criteria noted above.

The impact of technological change is the largest of the three countries with the expected large impact on the product life cycle. In the Bulgarian case this is not associated with increased customer choice or customisation and could be used instead to drive down costs and prices to an affordable level.

It is in Bulgaria that the key issue of distributor power noted for Hungary and Poland is absent. This is seen to reflect the small progress being made towards privatisation with little change expected in this area but does not mean that it is an unimportant issue.

5.2 Key Factors for Success

The previous sections have investigated the marketing environments in which companies in Hungary, Poland and Bulgaria are expected to operate in the next few years. The survey also studied the means by which companies felt that competitive advantage could be gained in these environments. This is important for determining where key interventions can be made.

Respondents were asked to rank order the factors that they believed were the keys to competitive success in their markets. The percentage of respondents ranking the individual factors first or second is shown in Table 2. The table shows both the total sample response and that for the three individual countries respectively.

5.2.1 Overall Results

The two dominant factors were competitive pricing (38%) and product quality (32%). The second of these reflects the marketing environment issues discussed above, the first is an indication that in a free market economy prices are no longer controlled and for the first time become an important source of competitive advantage. The importance of also achieving a cost advantage is not, however, recognised with only 8% mentioning this factor.

The second set of factors relates to improved customer relations and includes company/brand reputation (15%), speed of reaction to customer requirements (15%), product performance (14%), and close links with customers (14%). It is interesting that an increased awareness of the importance of the customers and their needs is seen as a key success factor. The relative importance of prior market research (10%) supports this view.

Other less important factors correspond with the traditional marketing mix factors ranging from product range offered (11%) to after sales service (2%).

Thus, overall, the freeing of the market has caused an emphasis on pricing and product quality, while there is an increased awareness of customer orientated issues. While this is true for the sample as a whole there are considerable differences in the responses for the individual countries which are discussed below.

5.2.2 Key Factors for Success in Hungary

The two first ranked factors of competitive pricing (53%) and product quality (45%) correspond with the overall sample responses where there is a need to provide good quality products at affordable prices. This is both a challenge for Hungarian companies and an opportunity for Western companies to invest. The identification of specific customer needs in the form of speed of reaction to customer requirements (17%) and close links with

Table 2. Key Factors for Marketing Success

KEY FACTORS FOR MARKET SUCCESS (percent ranking factor 1 or 2)	Total Sample (n = 2309)	Hungary (n = 893)	Poland (n = 893)	Bulgaria (n = 523)
Competitive Pricing	37.9%	52.7%	32.6%	21.6%
Product Quality	32.3%	44.6%	30.8%	13.8%
Company/Brand Reputation	15.2%	10.3%	22.1%	11.7%
Speed of Reaction to customer requirements	14.6%	17.1%	12.9%	13.2%
Product Performance	13.7%	11.3%	14.8%	16.1%
Close links with key customers	13.6%	17.1%	15.5%	2.7%
Product range offered	10.7%	5.5%	17.4%	8.0%
Prior Market Research	10.3%	2.8%	6.6%	29.3%
Product Design	9.1%	1.8%	15.8%	10.3%
Finance and Credit Offered	9.0%	5.5%	14.6%	5.5%
Distribution Coverage and/or uniqueness	7.7%	5.7%	8.1%	10.5%
A cost Advantage	7.6%	6.0%	10.1%	5.9%
Advertising	7.0%	2.1%	5.6%	17.6%
Personal Selling	6.8%	8.8%	5.7%	5.4%
Contacts throughout the Industry	5.5%	2.8%	10.6%	1.5%
Other promotions	4.9%	1.9%	4.1%	11.5%
Close links with industry suppliers	4.5%	2.7%	7.5%	2.7%
Superior marketing information systems	3.5%	3.0%	5.8%	0.4%
Superior Packaging	2.7%	1.5%	4.5%	1.9%
After sales Service	2.3%	2.8%	0.1%	5.2%

61

customers (17%) are next in order of priority ranked above company/product characteristics like reputation (10%) and product performance (14%). In industrial and service markets this is achieved through personal selling and it is interesting that of the marketing mix factors in Hungary there is an emphasis on personal selling (9%).

5.2.3 Key Factors for Success in Poland

Again the two top ranked factors were competitive pricing (33%) and product quality (31%). The next three most highly ranked factors focus on the company/product rather than on the customer needs. The factors concerned are: company/brand reputation (22%), product range offered (17%), and product design (16%). This could reflect a more product orientated approach rather than a customer orientated one (Hooley et al. 1993). A question must be raised here as to whether the responses represent the actual needs of the market place or whether they represent product orientated companies' views of the market place. This is an important question that needs to be answered by any Western company thinking of doing business in Poland.

5.2.4 Key Factors for Success in Bulgaria

The ranking of the success factors by the Bulgarian respondents was somewhat different from both the overall sample and the Hungarian and Polish samples. The top ranking factor was prior market research (29%). This is conventionally correct but is surprising in the context of the Bulgarian market place. It is, however, encouraging to note that its importance is recognised. The second most cited factor was competitive pricing (22%), in line with the responses from the other samples. The third most popular response was advertising (18%) and had much greater prominence than in the other samples. This corresponds with the selling orientation of Bulgarian marketing noted elsewhere (Hooley et al. 1993). This view is supported by the greater prominence of other promotions (12%) and took precedence over product performance (16%) and product quality (14%). The customer orientation in the form of speed of reaction to customer requirements was ranked only sixth (12%).

It is clear that in general the major key factors for success are competitive pricing and product quality but that beyond that there are key differences in the factors necessary for success in the individual countries. Hungary takes a more marketing orientated philosophy, Poland is more product orientated while Bulgaria is more selling orientated.

5.3 Competitive Edge

Respondents were asked to indicate whether or not they felt their companies had a Competitive Edge in each of the Key Factors for Success. These Key Factors for Success and Competitive Edge responses were combined into an "Opportunity Factor." Clearly an opportunity for Western intervention exists when there is no Competitive Edge corresponding to a first or second ranked Key Factor for Success. Similarly if the Competitive Edge and the first or second ranked Key Factor for Success coincide, the opportunity is already being met and a balanced situation exists.

Conversely, when a Competitive Edge exists corresponding to a Key Factor for Success not ranked first or second, "overkill" is taking place and resources are being wasted on unimportant issues. Obviously Western investment would not be appropriate in these circumstances. The final situation where there is no Competitive Edge in unimportant Key Factors for Success again provides no opportunity for investment from the outside. Table 3 shows the results of this analysis. The column labelled "Total" shows the percentage frequency of occurrence of the particular Competitive Edge. The other columns show the percentage frequency of each factor represented in each of the four categories: "Opportunity," "Balance," "Overkill," and "Unimportant." The most important opportunities for Western investment occur for the factors mentioned by the most respondents and where the "Opportunity" outweighs the "Overkill." The implications of this are discussed below.

5.3.1 The Opportunities

For the sample as a whole the main factors where the opportunities dominate are: competitive pricing where the opportunity frequency is 1.6 times greater than the overkill, product quality where the same factor is 1.5, product performance with a factor of 2.1, and prior market research with a factor of 1.5. These are clearly areas where Western help would be of value and where investment would be fruitful. Of particular interest are product performance and quality which are related and where Western expertise and technology could be of considerable help.

It is significant that the factors where the opportunities did not dominate focused mainly on good domestic relations, e.g., close links with customers with an opportunity to overkill ratio of 0.38, contacts throughout the industry with a ratio of 0.35, and close links with suppliers with a ratio of 0.38. These represent good local knowledge which can be exploited to improve the realisation of free market opportunities via the investment in the other areas indicated above.

TABLE 3. Competitive Advantage

COMPETITIVE EDGE	Total Sample (n = 2309)	Opportunity	Balance	Overkill	Not important
Competitive Pricing	34.3%	22.4%	17.8%	14.1%	45.7%
Product Quality	31.4%	20.7%	14.6%	13.8%	50.9%
Company/Brand Reputation	26.7%	11.1%	6.8%	17.0%	65.0%
Speed of Reaction to customer requirements	22.8%	10.0%	6.2%	15.1%	68.8%
Product Performance	9.5%	11.5%	3.2%	5.4%	79.9%
Close links with key customers	29.1%	8.1%	6.6%	21.3%	64.0%
Product range offered	19.4%	7.4%	4.6%	13.4%	74.6%
Prior Market Research	9.3%	9.6%	1.8%	6.4%	82.2%
Product Design	10.8%	6.9%	3.1%	6.8%	83.2%
Finance and Credit Offered	14.6%	7.7%	3.0%	10.0%	79.3%
Distribution Coverage and/or uniqueness	11.9%	5.7%	2.5%	8.9%	82.9%
A cost Advantage	11.7%	6.9%	2.4%	7.6%	83.1%
Advertising	8.7%	7.8%	0.8%	6.2%	85.2%
Personal Selling	12.6%	6.9%	2.2%	8.2%	82.7%
Contacts throughout the Industry	17.5%	4.9%	2.1%	13.9%	79.1%
Other promotions	5.5%	5.3%	0.5%	4.2%	90.0%
Close links with industry suppliers	13.3%	3.9%	1.8%	10.4%	83.9%
Superior marketing information systems	6.6%	3.2%	1.0%	5.0%	90.8%
Superior Packaging	4.2%	3.2%	0.3%	3.0%	93.4%
After sales service	4.5%	2.8%	0.7%	0.7%	93.9%

The same analysis was carried out for the individual countries which produced a very similar picture to this overall view. The only exception to this was that, in addition to the opportunities noted above, there was a considerable opportunity in Bulgaria to improve the distribution coverage where there was an opportunity to overkill ratio of 7.1.

6. CONCLUSIONS

The macro-environmental review has shown that the governments in the three countries are trying to address the problems associated with moving towards free market economies and in so doing have made them more attractive to Western investment by showing commitment to private investment and the promise of stability. They have also facilitated the exchange of currency and relaxed the laws concerning equity stakes in joint ventures. In this respect they have tried to move themselves from "cold" to at least "warm" countries in Goodnow and Hansz terminology. The general overall conclusion is that Hungary is the most attractive country in these terms with Bulgaria the least attractive and Poland occupying an intermediate position. The present research has looked in more detail at the market and competitive conditions in each country and has identified a number of opportunities for Western companies to invest in and help the three countries which add an extra dimension to the macro arguments.

The freeing of the markets has led to a demand for product quality, reliability and range. Western expertise and more efficient production methods could help in the provision of these from a lower cost base. The use of more sophisticated technology would facilitate this and provide a competitive edge via greater customisation. A second, very important issue is the need to develop the distribution channels. Here, again, Western companies have a great deal to offer to the mutual benefit of the company and the country.

There are important country specific differences in the changing market environment. In Hungary the changing needs include the provision of more customer choice, the need for more technological input to reduce costs at the same time as allowing this greater choice. In Poland, the environmental issues again centre on the need for more customisation and technological input. In Bulgaria these changes are present in the responses but there is a greater importance attached to the provision of quality and reliability and to the development of adequate distribution channels. The latter is seen as potentially having the greatest impact.

These changes in the market environment represent the challenges to which the countries have to respond.

The research has investigated what the key competitive issues are and where there is a need for improvement in the competitive position of respondent companies. Areas of relative weakness were competitive pricing, product quality and performance, and market research. Improvements in these areas would represent major opportunities to gain competitive advantage. It is also significant that the need for competitive pricing was not matched with an awareness of the need to reduce costs. This again would provide a sustainable competitive advantage. Additionally, in Bulgaria a major need is for a considerable improvement in the distribution channels.

Thus it is seen that, despite the obvious risks in investing in Hungary, Poland and Bulgaria, there are considerable opportunities that represent a chance of benefiting the countries concerned and of providing an investment opportunity for Western companies.

REFERENCES

Anderson E and Coughlan AT, (1987), International Market Entry and Expansion via Independent Integrated Channels of Distribution, *Journal of Marketing*, vol 51 pp. 71-82.

Bird J, (1992), Hungary's Appetite for Growth, *Management Today*, pp. 115-116.

Boudette NE, (1989), Europe's Horizons Spread Eastward, *Industry Week*, vol 238 No. 23 pp. 73-75.

Goodnow JD, (1985), Developments in International Mode of Entry Analysis, *International Marketing Review*, autumn, pp. 17-30.

Goodnow JD and Hansz JE, (1972), Environmental Determinants of Overseas Market Entry Strategies, *Journal of International Business Studies*, vol 3 No. 1 pp. 33-50.

Hooley GJ, Avlonitis G, Beracs J, Cox T, Fonfara K, Kolos K, Kouremenos T, Marinov M and Shipley D, (1993), A Comparative Study of Marketing in Hungary, Poland and Bulgaria, Proceedings of European Marketing Academy, Barcelona ESADE.

Klein S, Frazier GL and Roth VJ, (1990), A Transaction Cost Analysis Model of Channel Integration in International Markets, *Journal of Marketing Research*, vol 25, pp. 196-208.

Locher G, (1992), Europe's Changing Face, *Business Credit*, vol 94 No. 10 pp. 26-28.

Mann CL, (1991), Industrial Restructuring in East-Central Europe, *American Economic Review*, vol 81 No. 2 pp. 181-184.

Siren M and Shaw D, (1991), *Assessing the Market and the Opportunities*, vol 15 No. 2 pp. 30-33.

Weiner S, (1990), On the Road to Eastern Europe, *Forbes*, vol 146 No. 13 pp. 193-200.

Williams K, (1993), Can Western Investments in Eastern Europe Succeed? *Management Accounting*, vol 74 No. 8 p. 17.

Market Entry and Marketing Strategies for Eastern Europe

Reiner Springer

1. INTRODUCTION

Ever since the revolutionary developments of 1989 in Eastern Europe,[1] the conditions and principles for doing business have changed. This is especially true for the former socialist countries of Europe and the member states of the dissolved CMEA (successor states of the USSR, Bulgaria, Czech Republic, Slovak Republic, Poland, Hungary, and the former GDR).

The common economic feature of these states was a centralised planned economy with varying degrees of centralisation. All these states are currently in transition from a planned economy to a market economy.

This transition has very rapidly altered the marketing framework for Western companies in Eastern Europe and has led to questions which are of theoretical and practical interest. Some of these questions are:

- What are the development trends in the marketing environment in Eastern Europe?
- Which markets in Eastern Europe should be chosen and how can those markets be evaluated?
- What are the options for market entry?
- Which strategies should be favoured to penetrate the markets in Eastern Europe?

Reiner Springer is affiliated with Institut für BWL des Außenhandels, Wirtschaftsuniversität Wien, Althanstraße 51, A-1090 Wien, Austria.

[Haworth co-indexing entry note]: "Market Entry and Marketing Strategies for Eastern Europe." Springer, Reiner. Co-published simultaneously in *Journal of East-West Business* (International Business Press, an imprint of The Haworth Press, Inc.) Vol. 1, No. 3, 1995, pp. 67-104; and: *The Central and Eastern European Markets: Guideline for New Business Ventures* (ed: Petr Chadraba) International Business Press, an imprint of The Haworth Press, Inc., 1995, pp. 67-104. Single or multiple copies of this article are available from The Haworth Document Delivery Service [1-800-342-9678, 9:00 a.m. - 5:00 p.m. (EST)].

67

This article will analyse certain aspects of these questions, as well as the implementation of marketing theory in Eastern Europe. The aim is to verify the specifics of international marketing in economies of transition, and to develop conclusions for marketing strategies.[2]

2. MARKETING ENVIRONMENT IN EASTERN EUROPE

The shift from a planned economy to a market economy is connected with rapid and basic changes in the political, legal, economic, and financial conditions of doing business in all Eastern European countries. In Figure 1, basic changes in the marketing environment are summarised.

All countries in Eastern Europe are on the verge of introducing a market economy. According to Farrell,[3] the measures listed in Figure 2 are necessary to accomplish the shift from the planned economy to the market economy. The World Bank is recommending similar steps.[4] Principally, the reform programs of the countries in Eastern Europe contain these measures.

The duration of the transition, the sequence and the speed of the reform steps will differ from country to country, since each individual country has to decide between a sudden or gradual transition period. A pure shock therapy is very difficult to implement, since the political legitimacy of the reformers who are trying to transform the economy could be lost. The speed of transition must allow for the population to survive the transformation. Basically, all countries have opted for a gradual transition, although the speed of the reforms varies from country to country.

The transition to a market economy requires the abolishment of the planned economy bureaucracy and the reduction of central economic power. This deregulation leads to the liquidation of state monopolies in foreign trade and foreign currency management. Competition is being permitted as a prerequisite for a rational allocation of resources and an equal treatment of companies. The reformation of the price system, especially the liberalisation of prices and the reduction of subsidies, is a logical consequence of the abolishment of monopolies. Both measures are interlocked, since the liberalisation of prices would lead to nowhere, if monopolistic structures are not broken up. This results in a decentralisation of economic decisions, whereby the centre loses economic power and the companies gain a greater decision competence. The deregulation taking place brings about a new decision behaviour in companies and individual consumers.

Every market economy is based on private property. In Eastern Europe, private property in land and in the means of production was economically insignificant and strictly controlled by the state until 1989. The contribu-

FIGURE 1. Changes in the Marketing Environment in Eastern Europe

Political Environment	Legal Environment	Economic Environment	Cultural Environment
• democratisation of the society • pluralistic party system • freely elected parliaments • abolishment of centralist power structures	• juridical and legal reforms • new economic laws based on Western laws • change of people in legal apparatus	• step by step transition to a market economy • transformation crisis • privatisation • reforming money and banking system • permission of competition and abolishment or reduction of state monopolies • reforming price system and reduction of subsidies • going international • decentralisation of economic decision processes • demand markets and low competitiveness of Eastern suppliers • underdeveloped marketing infrastructure • positive transformation perspectives	• relative stability of cultural values • increasing influence of Western culture

FIGURE 2. From Socialism to Capitalism: Things to Do

Property Rights	Introduce private ownership laws differentiated by enterprise size and kind of property (housing, land); clarify the self-management and foreign ownership issues.
Competitive Markets	Eliminate central allocation and rationing; raise prices on necessities; free competitive sectors; establish anti-trust, contract and bankruptcy law; eliminate subsidies; remove redistribution pricing in favor of income-tested transfers; break up monopolistic firms; encourage foreign capital and small enterprises.
International	Remove quantitative restrictions and substitute tariffs; align different exchange rates; establish convertible currency.
Financial Sector	Free interest rates; separate commercial banking from central banking; establish interbank money market; lower entry barriers to financial sector; establish central bank independence and supervisory bodies for financial sector.
Labor Market	Free firms to lay off workers; introduce unemployment insurance, safety net, retraining and collective bargaining.
Hard Budget Constraints	Separate enterprises from the government; reform accounting; introduce rigorous profit and credit constraint; end tax and regulatory haggling; de-politicise firm behavior.
Stabilisation Policies	Reduce budget deficit; raise interest rates; employ anti-inflationary policies (tax-based incomes policies; foreign competition); regulate the money supply.
Management and Education	Train managers; educate populace (profit and competition); promote managers on basis of commercial achievement and make sure that the state managers follow profit-oriented policies.

70

tion of the private sector to the Gross National Product was between 20% in Poland and 2.5% in the former USSR.[5] Privatisation of state owned property, especially industrial and service enterprises, has begun in all countries of Eastern Europe. The degree of privatisation presently accomplished differs from country to country. Privatisation in East Germany will be completed by the end of 1994. In Poland, the Czech Republic and Hungary, the share of the private sector in the Gross Domestic Product is near 50%. In the other countries of Eastern Europe, privatisation is proceeding at a much slower pace. Patterns and steps of privatisation are similar in all countries and can be described as follows:

1. Change in the legal status of companies from a state owned status to a private legal status (formal privatisation).
2. Transfer of property titles to private investors (real privatisation).
3. Confronting the new owners with all commercial risks, cutting off or reducing state subsidies, and permitting bankruptcy.

Privatisation in Eastern Europe is gaining acceptance. The majority of Eastern Europeans are convinced that private entrepreneurs are better managers than the state, although the opinions differ from country to country (see Figure 3).

The transition from the planned economy to the market economy has caused a recession, which can be characterised as a transition crisis, in all countries of Eastern Europe. A sharp reduction in the Gross Domestic Product and industrial production, as well as increasing inflation rates and growing unemployment, are the statistical proof of this (for selected data see Figure 4).[6]

Important steps have been taken in the transition from a planned economy to a market economy in Eastern Europe. This is especially valid for Hungary, the Czech Republic, and Poland. Important results of this transformation are summarised in Figure 5.[7]

The progressing transformation will lead to a growing similarity in the market environment between countries in the industrialised West and in the East. The systemic differences between the two economic regions, which were typical in the past and are, still in part, existing today will disappear over time, as Figure 6 demonstrates. The higher the degree of compatibility in the marketing environment between Eastern Europe and the industrialised countries, the more attractive the new markets in the East will become.

3. THE NEED FOR MARKET SELECTION

The transformation in Eastern Europe has increased the number of markets in this region. New markets have emerged as a result of the

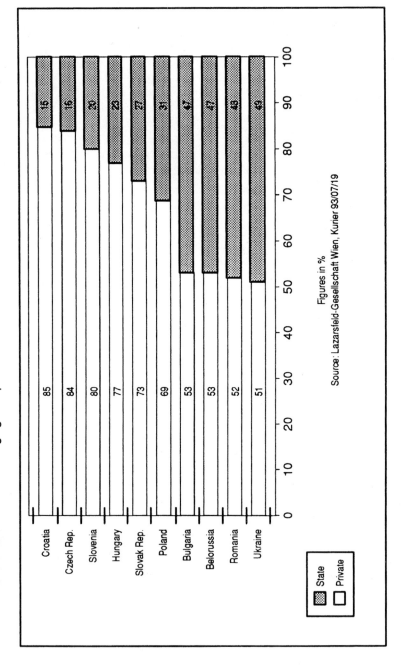

FIGURE 3. Who Is Managing Companies Better? Results of a Poll Taken in Eastern Europe

Figures in %
Source: Lazarsfeld-Gesellschaft Wien, Kurier 93/07/19

FIGURE 4. Economic Development in Eastern Europe, Russia, and the Ukraine

Annual Change in %	1990	1991	1992
GDP	-3,6	-10,2	-15,0
Eastern Europe	-7,2	-12,1	-6,5
East Middle Europe	-6,9	-10,6	-2,5
South East Europe	-7,7	-14,7	-14,0
Russia, Ukraine	-2,1	-9,5	-18,0
Industrial Production	-5,2	-13,3	-15,0
Eastern Europe	-15,3	-19,5	-11,0
East Middle Europe	-14,1	-17,5	-4,0
South East Europe	-17,1	-22,3	-21,0
Russia, Ukraine	-0,2	-10,3	-17,0
Construction Industry	-7,7	-12,1	-30,0
Eastern Europe	-15,7	-16,5	0,0
East Middle Europe	-11,6	-7,1	+9,0
South East Europe	-25,3	-38,1	-21,0
Russia, Ukraine	-5,2	-10,7	-39,0
Agriculture	-3,6	-6,5	-10,0
Eastern Europe	-3,3	-2,4	-13,0
East Middle Europe	-3,1	-3,0	-15,0
South East Europe	-3,5	-1,2	-11,0
Russia, Ukraine	-3,6	-7,5	-9,0

Eastern Europe: Bulgaria, CSFR, Croatia, Poland, Romania, Slovenia, Hungary
East Middle Europe: CSFR, Poland, Hungary
South East Europe: Bulgaria, Croatia, Romania, Slovenia

FIGURE 5. Status of the Economic Transition in Eastern Europe

Measure	Hungary	Poland	Czech Republic	Slovak Republic	Romania
Liberalisation of prices	finished	finished	finished	finished	partly finished
Liberalisation of foreign trade	almost accomplished	realised	almost accomplished	almost accomplished	partly finished
Macro economic regulation	sufficient regulation	partly regulated	sufficient regulation	planned	insufficient regulation
Small privatisation	almost finished	progressing very well	almost finished	almost finished	planned
Mass Privatisation	gradual	gradual	fast	gradual	isolated

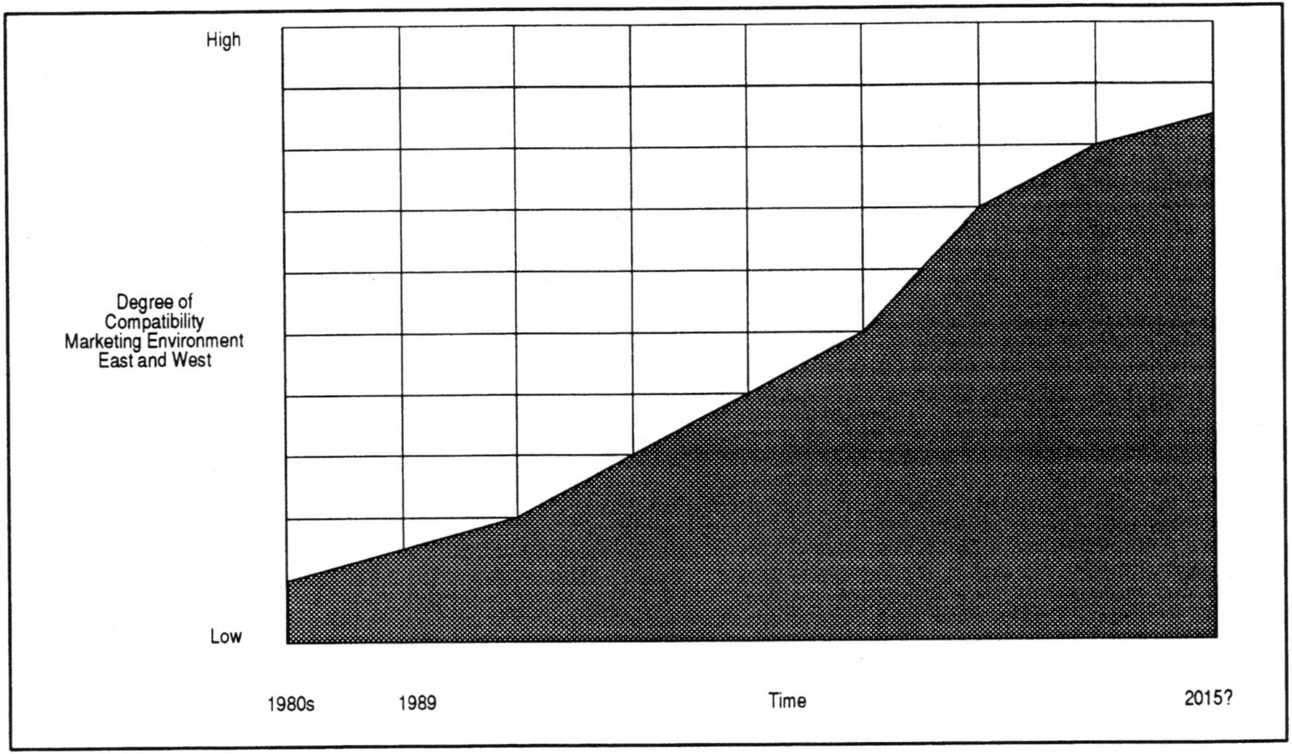

FIGURE 6. Development of the Marketing Environment in Eastern Europe

division of states. The nine former communist states, Albania, Bulgaria, CSSR, GDR, Hungary, Poland, Romania, USSR, and Yugoslavia, have split into 27 new democratic states.

The aim of market selection is to find the relevant markets for a company. Through market selection, potential customers and competitors can be determined. Based on the methods of market selection described in other literature,[8] decision oriented market selection models like checklists, point evaluation, and country portfolio are best qualified for the country market selection in Eastern Europe. The implementation of these models depends mainly on the availability of the necessary data.

The basic principle of these methods is the evaluation of markets by one or several criteria, which allow for the ranking of the countries and helps to facilitate the selection decision. In general, the selection criteria are related to the marketing environment, market access, market potential and competition.

Implementation of the Checklist-Method

A checklist contains criteria that must be met by the chosen country market. If all criteria are fulfilled, then the prerequisites are given to engage in the market. Market selection in Eastern Europe can be based on the criteria in Figure 7.

Very often, it will suffice to use only some of the above listed criteria. Important criteria are transformation perspectives, privatisation success, import barriers, availability and effectiveness of distribution channels, and market potential.

Implementation of the Point Evaluation

The point evaluation method quantifies qualitative judgements. The selection decision is based on the total number of points that the different markets achieve. The point evaluation can be carried out with the criteria presented in Figure 8.

Market Selection by Portfolio

Market selection by portfolio means positioning markets with the help of different criteria for the use of comparison and analysis. In graphical form the axles are often "Market attractiveness" and "Political stability/ Risk Potential."[9] In regard to Eastern Europe, the sub-criteria of "Market capacity" and "Commercial risk" are very important.

Market attractiveness is mainly determined by market potential and

FIGURE 7. Criteria for Market Selection in Eastern Europe with the Checklist-Method

Environment	Market Access	Market Capacity	Competition
• economic reforms • transformation perspectives • privatisation success • acceptance of the economic reforms by the population	• import barriers • export regulations • certification procedure • distribution infrastructure	• market potential • market growth • sales volume • market share • general sales conditions	• market share • customers • services • marketing concept • market entry mode

FIGURE 8. Criteria for Market Selection in Eastern Europe Using the Point Evaluation Method

Criteria	Sub-Criteria (examples)
market potential/ market capacity	• total potential demand • population • GNP/GDP • household income/investments
market growth	estimates for • GDP-development • investments • income development
market volume	• sales volume by industry branch • state budget • purchasing power
market access	• possible market entry modes • foreign trade system • incentives for foreign investors
transformation perspective	• progress of economic reforms • abolishment of state monopolies • degree of decentralisation and deregulation • inflation, reduction of deficits in the state budget

privatisation success	• share of private sector in BIP • conditions for the participation of foreigners in privatisation • options for buying real estate
legal framework	• status of legal reform • equal treatment of foreign companies
distribution conditions	• availability of distribution channels • transportation and logistic systems
intensity of competition	• competition from abroad • domestic competition • prerequisites for fair competition
commercial risks	• contract risk • customer risk • payment risk • credit risk • product risk • distribution risk • price risk • inflation risk • acceptance risk

market capacity. Market capacity is the total real and potential demand in a market[10] and also comprises the future demand in Eastern Europe, which is currently not being covered by purchasing power. Precisely this potential demand is very important in regard to the selection of markets to be entered, because with the current transitional progress, the purchasing power will increase and potential demand will turn into real demand.

The risk potential can be divided into political and economic risk. Political risks are considered low, since the reforms in Eastern Europe are irreversible. The economic risk is difficult to operationalise. One possibility is to evaluate the commercial risk. Commercial risks are all risks which may occur during the realisation process of a foreign trade contract with companies in Eastern Europe. This definition states that there is a distinction between country risk[11] and commercial risk. Country risks and commercial risks are risks of different dimensions. A given country risk does not necessarily determine a commercial risk. On the other hand, a commercial risk can exist so that even a low risk for a certain country is assumed. Normally, a company is not dealing with an Eastern European country as a whole, but with individual companies within the country. Therefore, a company has to determine whether the contract in question can be realised without risks. Further, it must be determined whether a risky country market is also a risk for individual business deals.

The probability of commercial risks is different from country to country and varies according to the type of contract construction chosen.

In doing business with Eastern Europe the commercial risks listed in Figure 9A are especially of interest.

Figure 9B shows a portfolio for a selected group of Eastern European countries. The portfolio is based on the dimensions "Market attractiveness" and "Risk Potential." The market attractiveness was evaluated with the criteria purchasing power (weight 35%) GDP (30%), GDP per capita (20%), and Population (15%). A scale of 1 to 10 was used, whereby 1 means low market attractiveness and 10 high market attractiveness. The dimension risk potential was evaluated with the criteria legal security (weight 50%), creditworthiness (40%), and inflation (10%). On the scale, 1 means high risk potential and 10 low risk potential. If available, data for the years 1989 to 1992 were used, while figures for 1993 and beyond were estimated.

4. MARKET ENTRY MODES

Economic reforms and liberalisation of foreign trade have opened the markets in Eastern Europe, which can now be entered by all known entry modes. In the past, the markets in Eastern Europe could only be entered by

FIGURE 9A. Commercial Risks in Trading with Eastern Europe

Risk	Problem area
Contract risk	Non-compatibilty of commercial laws in Eastern Europe with international laws, implementaion of different trade rules. Arbitrary system unknown.
Customer risk	Liquidation of companies can cause disturbances in supplier customer relations.
Payment risk	Bankruptcy in the process of privatisation
Credit risk	Limited access to international foreign trade financing. Change in credit conditions of Eastern European banks.
Product risk	Technological compatibility questionable.
Distribution risk	Limited efficiency of national distribution systems.
Price risk	Danger of price regulation in response to resistance of economic reforms.
Inflation risk	Hyperinflation, difficulties to calculate prices on a long-term basis.
Acceptance risk	Reservations against Western companies and managers, especially in connection with privatisation.

FIGURE 9B. Country Portfolio Eastern Europe

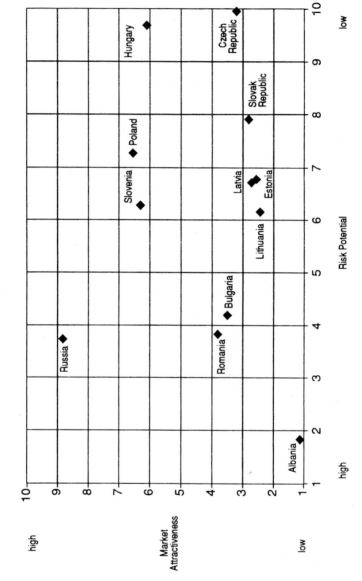

export or through joint ventures in some countries (Poland, Hungary, Romania). Now, all possible entry modes can be pursued: export, direct investment, licensing, production by contract, and management by contract. Due to the economic insecurities in these markets caused by the transition crisis, many Western companies favour a more traditional approach to these markets, starting with export and import. A company, which is concentrating on exporting only, might miss unique opportunities for direct investments, and therefore strategic acquisitions, which exist as a result of the ongoing privatisation. The decision for export or direct investment depends mainly on company targets and the concrete marketing environment. In a survey of 337 Austrian companies, 56% have opted for export first, 36% rely on acquisitions, and 22% believe in the establishment of subsidiaries (multiple answers possible).[12]

The advantages and disadvantages of the entry modes, export and direct investment, in Eastern Europe are summarised in Figure 10.

Market Entry by Export and Import

The abolishment of the foreign trade monopoly and the right of Eastern companies to engage in foreign trade on their own has opened new options for Western companies in channel management. Western companies are no longer forced to channel all their exports and imports through state owned Foreign Trade Organisations (FTOs).[13]

Import Channels

In the past, imports from Eastern countries had to be channelled through FTOs. Normally, there was only one seller, since the FTOs had been structured according to the principle "one product–one FTO." The Western buyer was unable to choose between several suppliers.

After the abolishment of the foreign trade monopoly, foreign companies can now choose between four import channels:

1. Direct import from the manufacturer in Eastern Europe;
2. Import through the Trading Houses of Manufacturers;
3. Import through Trading Houses functioning as intermediaries for several manufacturers;
4. Import through Export Co-operatives or Trade Associations of small and medium sized companies.

The possibilities for direct imports will enlarge if manufacturers in Eastern Europe develop the prerequisites for their direct exports. Howev-

FIGURE 10. Comparison of the Market Entry Modes, Export and Direct Investment, in Eastern Europe

	Export		Direct investment	
	Advantage	Disadvantage	Advantage	Disadvantage
	low marketing costs	weak market position	different forms of economic co-operation possible	long-term engagement in the market
	low risks	low profits	normally higher financial results	high market investment
	fast results	displacement by competitors easily possible	better control of operation and decision taking	dependence on political and economic environment in the market
	change of customers easily possible	delivery and distribution risk	potential for widening the market position	difficulties in gaining and implementing owner's rights

er, in the near future, many companies will have to rely on Trading Houses for exports, since they themselves lack the necessary export know-how.

Export Channels

Under the presence of the foreign trade monopoly, exports into the markets of Eastern Europe were channelled through FTOs, as Figure 11 shows. The FTOs distributed the commodities to the domestic end users. Normally, the foreign supplier did not have access to the end user.

After the liberalisation of the foreign trade system, several export channels opened up to Western suppliers:

1. Direct export to the end user, especially in regard to industrial products.
2. Export through Trading Houses, which operate as intermediaries (dealer or agent) and establish direct contacts between foreign suppliers and domestic end users.
3. Export to wholesalers and/or retailers, whereby Trading Houses can be part of the distribution chain.
4. Export through subsidiaries or joint ventures of Western companies in Eastern Europe, which serve end users or function as channel members.

Figure 12 gives an overview of the different channels to be used for exporting to Eastern Europe.

Direct Investments in Eastern Europe

Economic and political reforms in Eastern Europe offer various possibilities for Western companies to invest in this region (acquisition of

FIGURE 11. Export Channels into Eastern Europe Under the Presence of the Foreign Trade Monopoly

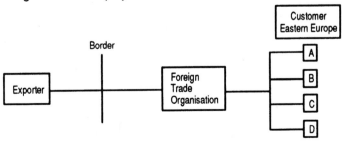

FIGURE 12. Export Channels into Eastern Europe

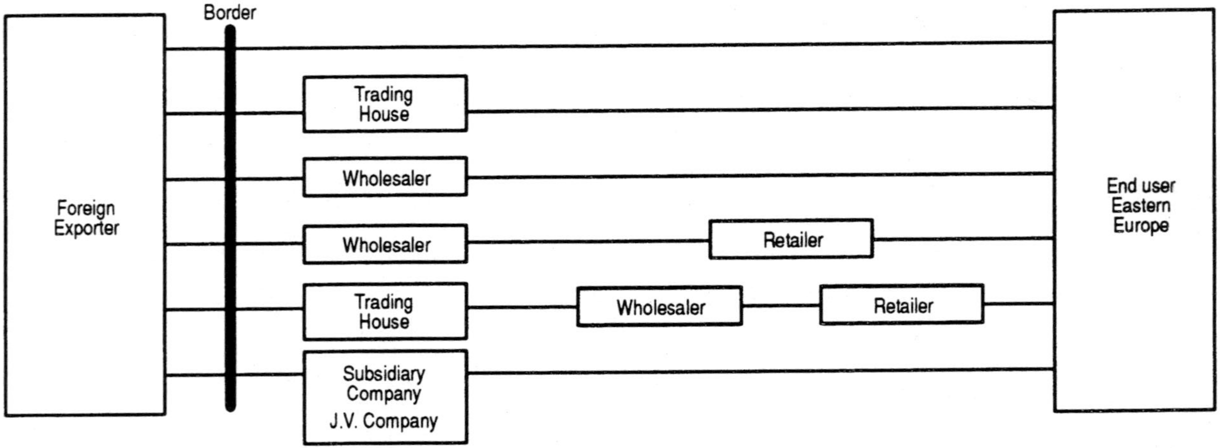

companies, green field investments, joint ventures). Privatisation results in a dominance of Buy-Strategies (acquisitions) compared to Build-Strategies or investment forms realised in the past such as joint ventures.

The economic conditions in Eastern Europe are more favourable for strategic investors. Financial investors cannot expect a quick return on investment. Strategic investments are promising for the following reasons:[14]

- securing of market shares: the acquisition of companies means buying market share, since Eastern European manufacturers of consumer products hold market shares of up to 90% in the domestic markets;
- access to material (raw materials, real estate) and human (research and development capacities) resources;
- positioning in an economic region with large market potential;
- development of competitive advantages due to low labour costs and preferable investment conditions;
- neutralisation of competitors.

Acquisitions in Eastern Europe are connected with various problems, such as:[15]

- *Development of feasibility studies and evaluation of companies:* The development of feasibility studies can be costly and time consuming because of insufficient data. The feasibility study should cover such typical areas as project evaluation, cost and use analysis, profitability analysis, chance and risk assessment. Special attention should be directed towards project background, estimation of potential sales, availability of production factors, technological standards for equipment, qualification and motivation of the workforce, dimension of the administrative apparatus, demands of the municipal authorities, and the capability of management.[16] The typical shortcomings of Eastern companies rests with non-competitive products, low productivity, high vertical integration, debt and insufficient liquidity and weak management.
  The evaluation of Eastern companies is rather difficult due to the lack of reliable balance sheets. The real book value of the companies can hardly be determined since a real estate market does not exist. The turnover of the past is not a valid yardstick for cash flow estimates since most of the markets of Eastern companies have dispersed.
- *Contract design:* The main partners for contract negotiations are the state agencies responsible for privatisation. Potential investors have to present comprehensive concepts for the companies to be acquired. These concepts will be assessed by the privatisation agencies mainly on the basis of such criteria as investments promised, jobs guaranteed and

buying price offered. Essential elements of the contract negotiation are the clarification of possible restitution claims, the take-over of ecological burdens and the handling of the indebtedness of companies.

*   *Reconstruction of Eastern companies:* A special challenge in the acquisition process is the rehabilitation of the Eastern company and its integration into the acquiring company. Reconstruction includes such tasks as a reduction of product assortment, a cutback of vertical integration, the establishment of a competitive distribution system, a quick increase in productivity, a reduction in insufficient use of material and energy, an improvement in product quality, product design and packaging, a reduction of administrative personnel, and the qualification and motivation of the workforce.

5. MARKETING MANAGEMENT IN EASTERN EUROPE

5.1. Basic Marketing Strategies

After the decision to enter the Eastern markets has been reached, the basic marketing strategy must be developed and the Marketing-Mix must be designed.

Marketing strategies are directed to achieve sustainable competitive advantages.[17] Such sustainable competitive advantages differ from country to country and from branch to branch and can be accomplished in Eastern Europe if companies base their strategies on the following considerations:

*   low price strategy;
*   offering of advantageous financing;
*   adaptation of products and services to be delivered to the needs and technological requirements of the customers in Eastern Europe;
*   presence in the markets, offering of complete assortments and services, take-over of distribution activities (storage, transportation, logistics, financing, consulting);
*   acceptance of countertrade.

In connection with the development of marketing strategies, the question of whether to pursue standardisation or differentiation must be dealt with. Eastern Europe is no longer a unique bloc and the ongoing transformations are deepening the differentiation between countries. Therefore, a differentiation strategy is more suited towards the inhomogeneous market requirements of the customers in these countries.

5.2. Marketing Research in Eastern Europe

Knowledge about the markets in Eastern Europe has improved over the last years, but is still not sufficient for many marketing decisions. The information base is inadequate for the following reasons:

- limited availability of reliable historical data;
- lack of detailed data;
- deficient compatibility of data compared with data from industrialised countries;
- shortcomings in the data stability because of ongoing structural and organisational changes of information sources;
- difficult access to primary information of end users.

Information availability and access differ from country to country. Figure 13 summarises the prevailing assessment in this regard.

In the past, market research in Eastern Europe was based on collecting and processing secondary market information. Possibilities to gather primary information (i.e., through panels and polls) has begun only during the past few years. The conditions for market research are improving rapidly: New information sources are available, market research institutions are offering their services, and trade associations are publishing more and more detailed data.

The competence and services of market research institutes in Eastern Europe are improving. This is primarily based on the growing co-operation between Western and Eastern market research institutes. The advantages for Western companies to use these joint institutes lie in the following reasons:[18]

- the search for an efficient institute becomes easier, the evaluation of unknown institutes can be avoided, since the Western partner is normally known;
- briefing and control will be easier because of the implementation of common research methods;
- language misunderstandings are being reduced;
- the implementation of Western market research know-how is being guaranteed.

The quality of estimates of future market trends depends heavily on the quality of market data. The method of "regional lead-lag analysis"[19] is a valuable instrument for forecasts due to the described data problems. By using this method, it is assumed that demand development in Eastern Europe will follow the known pattern of the highly developed countries.

FIGURE 13. Information Availability in Eastern Europe

Hungary Poland Czech Republic Slovak Republic	High Information Availability
Russia Bulgaria Romania Albania	Low Information Availability

5.2. Changes in Buying Behaviour

The transformation from a planned economy to a market economy causes changes in consumer and organisational buying behaviour. Typical for Eastern Europe is a growing differentiation in the buying behaviour of country markets, and even market segments within the countries. Over the long run, the buying behaviour in Eastern Europe will adjust to the buying behaviour in the industrialised countries.

Buying Behaviour of Consumers

The buying behaviour of consumers is determined by economic and non-economic factors. The non-economic factors can be grouped into social variables (family members, opinion leaders, culture, social class, impact of mass communication) and psychic variables (needs, emotions, attitudes, realisations, learning).[20]

Of special importance within the group of non-economic factors, in regard to the buying behaviour of consumers in Eastern Europe, is the buying experience. As far as the economic factors are concerned, purchasing power and supply have formed the buying behaviour.

Limited purchasing power and continuous shortages in supply have led to an economically determined buying behaviour.[21] Consumers hardly compared quality and prices, and as soon as the products reached the shelves they were bought in order to buy something at all. Price played a subordinated role in the buying decision due to the fact that purchasing power was larger than supply. However, these conditions have now changed. Money is limited and supply is broadening. The limited purchasing power, which is typical for all Eastern European countries, has meant that price has become a decisive buying factor.

The main features of the buying behaviour of consumers in Eastern Europe can be summarised in the following points:[22]

- Reduction of consumption because of the increase of prices and limited purchasing power;
- careful comparison of offers of different suppliers;
- avoidance of risky or quick buys;
- preparation of buying decisions in the family;
- stringent adaptation of personal purchasing power needs;
- increased brand consciousness;
- thorough price observation.

Organisational Buying Behaviour

In all countries of Eastern Europe, a shift in the hierarchy of organisational buying behaviour can be observed. Buying decisions, formerly taken on the level of the central state and planning apparatus, are now being taken by companies (end users) gaining economic independence. In Eastern Europe, company external buying centres (State Planning Commission, Ministries, Foreign Trade Organisations, Foreign Trade Bank) have especially dominated the buying decision of importers. As a result of the economic reforms, the buying decisions are increasingly taken by internal company buying centres. Therefore, it is important to determine the buying centre within the company, in order to contact their members directly. This is difficult, insofar as the organisational structure of the economy and companies, as well as the management personnel, is still undergoing changes.

Companies in Eastern Europe are undertaking their buying decisions on the basis of task oriented buying decision models. Buying decisions are generally based on the following criteria:

1. quality and technological compatibility of the products;
2. price;
3. competitive financing and acceptance of counter trade.

Changes in the organisational buying behaviour can be demonstrated with the results of a study of the buying behaviour of end users and importers of industrial equipment in former CSFR.[23]

Between May and July 1991, 40 industrial companies were questioned regarding their organisational buying behaviour. These 40 companies were a representative sample of Czech and Slovak companies importing industrial products from the West. Questionnaires were returned by 45% of the companies. At the time of the survey, 56% of the companies had purchased, for the first time since the political changes of 1989, industrial products from Western countries.

The Czech and Slovak companies are using the typical information sources to prepare the buying decisions, as Figure 14 shows. Contacts to suppliers, checking leaflets and exploiting buying experiences with potential suppliers are the most important sources for information.

The personnel composition of the buying centre is dominated by management in the case of a first time buy situation. In the case of a repeated purchase, technicians are the majority. Before 1990, the buying centre was controlled by top management (60%), but since that time technicians have been gaining influence (management still has 44.5%, technicians 33.3% and commercial staff 22.2%). In general, one should be aware that the personnel composition of the buying centres in Eastern Europe will constantly change over the next few years in connection with the privatisation and structural changes in the economy.

The ranking of the buying criteria is shown in Figure 15. The most important buying criterion is product quality, followed by price and guarantee conditions. The ranking of price as a dominant buying factor is due to the limited purchasing power of companies and their restricted access to convertible currencies.

5.3. Marketing-Mix Decisions

Product Policy for the Markets in Eastern Europe

The product policy for the markets in Eastern Europe is essentially determined by the technological gap between Western industrialised countries and the former Socialist countries in Eastern Europe. The meaning of the model outlining the technological gap for international trade has been extensively documented in the literature.[24] This model is based on the idea that a company in country A, which does have a technological advantage in a given product field, can profitably and basically without competition, export to target markets, as long as, manufacturers in these markets, or other competitors do not have the same know-how. This assumption is valid for Eastern Europe because most of these countries are decades behind the technological standard of the West. The conclusion is that the product life cycle, of many industrial products and technical consumer goods offered and traded on Western markets, has not yet begun in the Eastern markets or is only in the early phases.

Berekoven proves this point by stating that products, which have reached saturation in the domestic market, can still be new and attractive products in markets of a lower development level, due to the unavailability of information, lack of purchasing power and underdeveloped demand.[25]

From this starting point, product policy directed at Eastern markets

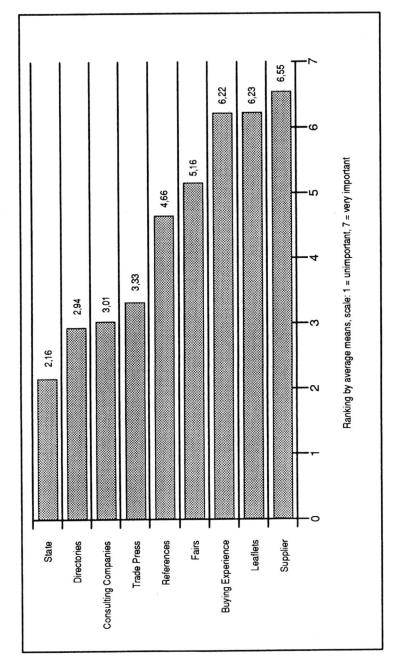

FIGURE 14. Information Sources Used in Organisational Buying Behaviour of Czech and Slovak Companies

Ranking by average means, scale: 1 = unimportant, 7 = very important

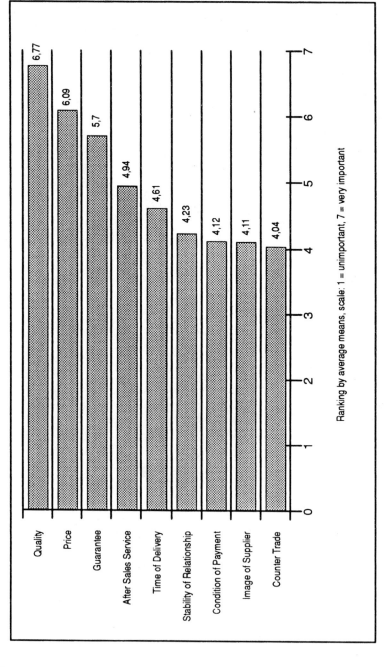

FIGURE 15. Buying Criteria Used in Organisational Buying Behaviour of Czech and Slovak Companies

Ranking by average means, scale: 1 = unimportant, 7 = very important

must select those products from the company's existing supply which are suitable for the markets of Eastern Europe. Eventually, the adaptation of the selected products is necessary. Therefore, product policy decisions for markets in Eastern Europe can be ranked by the following steps:

1. selection of products from the existing company supply for the export to or production in Eastern Europe;
2. adaptation of the selected products to the needs of the customers in Eastern Europe;
3. determination and realisation of product related services;
4. research of user problems in order to find ideas for new products.

Product policy decisions in regard to the markets in Eastern Europe are, at first, decisions to position established products in these markets. In Figure 16 questions are listed which should be answered if a product policy for Eastern Europe is going to be developed.

Marketing Communication in Eastern Europe

Marketing communication is of increasing importance in Eastern Europe. The liberalisation of foreign trade in these countries has widened the options for Eastern companies to trade with Western companies. Trade with the West is no longer state planned and companies must now decide for themselves with whom and under which conditions they want to do business. The companies in Eastern Europe can make those decisions only if they have enough information on potential partners in the West. Marketing communication has to take into account that Eastern companies have a huge information deficit regarding potential trading partners in foreign countries for primarily two reasons. Firstly, the Eastern companies have been separated from the world market for many years, and secondly, organisational changes in connection with privatisation have created new companies that are considering internationalisation for the first time.

Marketing communication in Eastern Europe must therefore, above all, reduce the information deficit regarding potential customers. The communication strategy needs to be based on the concrete market situation. Marketing communication in Eastern Europe uses well known communication instruments, which can be ranked in the following order:

1. Advertising;
2. Personnel Selling;
3. Public Relations;
4. Sales Promotion.

FIGURE 16. Checklist Product Policy Eastern Europe

Product:	Country:
Question/Evaluation Criteria	Answer/Evaluation
1. How will the market potential develop?	
2. Which quantities can our company sell?	
3. Will the customers accept our products?	
4. What is the relationship between world market prices and prices in the target market?	
5. Will the number and structure of customers change? What are the possible consequences for our sales volume?	
6. Have we to expect threats by our competitors?	
7. Can our company use distributors in the target market? Does their efficiency correspond with our marketing goals?	
8. Is our service sufficient to compete in the target market?	
9. What innovative and technological advantage do we have? When and how must the offered products be improved or adapted?	
10. What impact do trade barriers have?	

Advertising is the most important communication instrument in Eastern Europe.[26] Advertising in Eastern Europe, especially the formulation of the advertising message, is strongly influenced by the general economic conditions. Under the conditions of a seller's market, advertising should at first not create demand, but build up the brand name and prepare the market. This can be realised if company and product advertising are combined.

Experiences, especially in the advertising for consumer goods in Eastern Europe, can be summarised as follows:

- The success of advertising depends largely on the direct addressing of the targets, since customers in Eastern Europe react more sensitively to advertising messages than customers in industrialised countries.
- Consumers are interested in a rational advertising which clearly states its message. The customers expect that advertising should help them in sorting through numerous and confusing offers. Too much animation at the expense of information creates mistrust and builds up a psychic distance to the product.
- Advertising in television is not as accepted as advertising in the daily press. TV-advertising is considered too general and does not meet the information requirements of customers. Ads in papers, especially with informative and well structured argumentation, are being used to prepare buying decisions.
- The development and introduction of brands should be an essential part of any advertising campaign, since brand consciousness in Eastern Europe is underdeveloped. Branding strategies should take into account that domestic brands do not all have a poor image. In such cases, sensitive treatment of domestic brands is necessary in order not to offend domestic customers.

Based on the peculiarities in the buying behaviour, the question to be raised is whether a special advertising campaign should be pursued in Eastern Europe or whether strategies successfully implemented in Western markets are applicable. Both approaches are possible, as long as the advertising strategy takes into account the information needs of the customers in Eastern Europe. Practical experience shows that adjusted Western strategies can be implemented very successfully.

The advertising market in Eastern Europe is developing very quickly. In Hungary, the advertising expenditures increased from 5.6 billion Forint in 1991 to 11.6 billion Forint (215 Million DM) in 1992; the respective figure for the former CSFR in 1992 was 2.7 billion Czech Crowns (160 Million DM).[27]

Despite this increase, the advertising expenditures per capita in Hungary and in former CSFR are still below the level in Western countries, as a comparison with Austria in Figure 17 shows.

Channel Management

Channel decisions should be based on an evaluation of the features of the distribution conditions in Eastern Europe. In general, such an evaluation of target markets can be, according to Specht,[28] divided into group features and single features. By using this approach, an evaluation of the distribution conditions in Eastern Europe is presented in Figure 18.

The channel design should be based on careful consideration of the available options, whereby the following questions should be asked:

- Is direct export possible? What advantages and disadvantages does direct export have? Many customers in Eastern Europe, especially buyers of industrial products, have an interest in direct imports. Domestic intermediaries, above all the former state-owned FTOs, are being avoided. Therefore, the establishment of direct links to end users is not difficult. A problem that arises is that some of the end users do not have any experience with foreign trade. If this is the case, then direct links can be risky. In case of doubt, the services of a Trading House should be used, thereby still allowing for the development of direct connections to end users.

- Which intermediaries are available to establish a functioning multi-step distribution channel? Can such a channel be controlled by the Western company? Potential intermediaries are Trading Houses or the new private trading firms. Nevertheless, one has to be aware of the different prerequisites of private wholesalers and retailers in the countries of Eastern Europe.[29] In the successor states of the former USSR, a functioning wholesale trade system does not exist. Commodity exchanges are taking over the functions of wholesalers, as well as those of retailers. The retail system is very underdeveloped. For instance, per capita, only half as many shops exist in the former USSR as in Hungary.

- Which distributive functions must be offered in the Eastern markets? Due to the developing stage of the distribution system, companies exporting to these markets should be prepared to offer a whole range of distribution functions, such as selling, buying, financing, risk management, keeping a wide assortment, transportation, storage, logistics, packaging, market research, communication, and after sales services.

- How should channel members be positioned regionally in Eastern Europe? Deregulation of trade and the necessity to establish close contacts to the end users requires sales offices to be located near the customers. The concentration of sales representatives only in the capitals was sufficient in the past, since the customers (mainly FTOs) were located there.

Contractual Policy

The ongoing transformation means that the framework for contractual and pricing decisions is constantly changing. Customer and supplier relations are being reorganised. New customers are entering the market. Stable supplier-customer relationships have yet to be developed. The new legal framework is opening the way towards a wide variety of contract types and contract conditions. Financing of foreign trade operations is sometimes difficult due to the limited purchasing power of customers. Some partners in Eastern Europe are inexperienced in foreign trade.

These conditions require a careful negotiation of foreign trade contracts, especially in regard to risk management, selection of contract type and condition of payment. Contractual policy in Eastern Europe should address the following problems:

- Continual evaluation of the capacity and efficiency of unknown enterprises. The rapid changes in Eastern Europe require the constant observation of customers in order to recognise upcoming difficulties at an early stage. Passive research is not sufficient due to the time lags in the transfer of information. Most important is to have steady and direct contact with the trading partner in the East. Only market presence can ensure that market opportunities will be used and risks minimised. Personal contact with top management in the emerging companies creates a confidential basis that is necessary under these changing conditions.
- Changes in the ownership of companies, in management, and in the buying centres of the potential customers must be registered very carefully in order to maintain contact with the appropriate parties.
- The reliability and the creditworthiness of customers must be evaluated. This might include asking banking institutions for information.
- The decision between a low price strategy and a high price strategy must be based on the specific market conditions, the target groups envisioned, and the company objectives. For most standardised mass products, a low price strategy seems to be the right market oriented strategy due to the limited purchasing power. A growing number of customers

are ready and able to pay higher prices, especially for high quality technical products. In this case, a high price strategy would prove to be profitable in the future with the increase in purchasing power.
- The agreement of low risk contracts should be considered at the outset, especially in regard to the conditions of payment.
- A steady and early control of the fulfillment of foreign trade contracts by the Eastern partner seems to be necessary.

The major problem of the contractual policy in Eastern Europe is to find mutually agreeable financial arrangements. Classical forms of foreign trade financing are available on a limited scale only. The main problem is the limited purchasing power of potential customers, primarily due to the restricted access to convertible currencies or the limited liquidity.

Solutions exist in the following directions:

- project bound financial help by Western investors;
- use of export insurance systems;
- foreign trade financing through countertrade contracts.

Countertrade remains an important instrument of contract policy in Eastern Europe. Basically, all types of countertrade can be used in trading with Eastern European countries. Some examples are: Counter Purchase, Parallel Barter, Buy-Back, Compensation Arrangements, Clearing Account Barter, Offset-Deals, and Debt Swaps.

The complicated nature of countertrade operations requires that these transactions are often handled by specialists. Trading houses and banks can be of invaluable help to inexperienced companies.

CONCLUSION

The economic region of Eastern Europe is characterised by a growing differentiation in the political, economic, legal, and institutional conditions for doing business. The "old" and the "new" countries of Eastern Europe cannot be treated as a unique economic bloc, for which a standardised marketing strategy can be implemented. Successful marketing strategies have to be tailored to the specific requirements of these country markets. Market selection and segmentation, as well as a customer oriented Marketing-Mix-policy, are important tools to develop and realise appropriate strategies.

Market entry decisions are becoming more complex, which, in turn, requires the implementation of suitable decision procedures. The established methods of market selection and the various market entry modes are

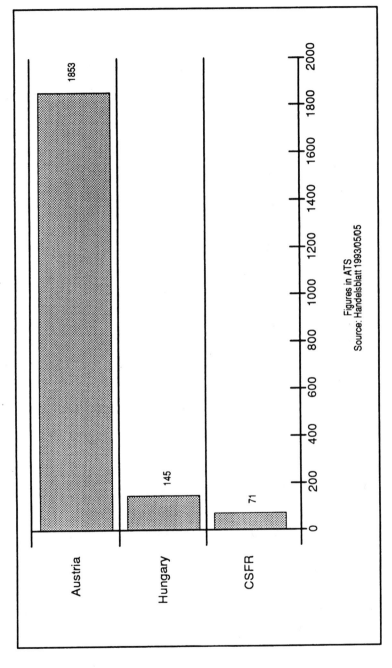

FIGURE 17. Advertising Expenditures Per Capita in Austria, Hungary, and CSFR 1992

Figures in ATS
Source: Handelsblatt 1993/05/05

FIGURE 18. Distributive Features of Target Markets in Eastern Europe

Group Feature	Single Feature
Market Type/Market Potential	• in general seller's market • huge demand for almost all products • deregulation of foreign trade and domestic buyer-seller-relations • shortcomings in the infrastructure, need for complex distribution systems
Customer Profile	• companies becoming economically independent • withdrawal of state as a buyer • underdeveloped wholesale and retail trade
Buying Behaviour	• price-performance-ratio decisive • industrial products from the West are preferred • big demand for services
Competitive Situation	• still developing • more competition between foreign than domestic suppliers

also applicable in Eastern Europe, but they must be modified in relation to the status of the transition process. The need for modifications will decline as the transition from a planned economy to a market economy continues.

NOTES

1. The term Eastern Europe has been used until the end of the 80s to mark the communist states in Europe. With the progressing transformation this meaning is becoming obsolete. In the context of the article the regional characterisation of this group of states is meant.

2. See also Springer, R.: Markteintrittsentscheidungen für Osteuropa, Marketing-Zeitschrift für Theorie und Praxis, No. 4, 1993.

3. Farrel, J. P.: Monitoring the Great Transition. In: Comparative Economic Studies, Vol. XXXIII, No. 2, Summer 1991, p. 13.

4. World Bank: The Transformation of Economies in Central and Eastern Europe: Issues, Progress, and Prospects. Washington 1991.

5. Schmieding, H./Koop, M. J.: Privatisierung in Mittel-und Osteuropa: Konzepte für den Hindernislauf zur Marktwirtschaft, Institut für Weltwirtschaft Kiel, February 1991.

6. Compiled from Gabrisch, H. u. a.: "Die Rezession schwächt sich ab-Die Wirtschaftslage in den post-sozialistischen Ländern Europas 1992/93," WIIW, Sonderdruck aus WIFO-Monatsberichte, 66. Jahrgang, Heft 5, 1993, Übersichten 1 bis 4.

7. Junge, G.: "Reformen tragen erste Früchte," Bankverein, Der Monat 6/93, p. 14.

8. For an overview see Breit, J.: Die Marktselektionsentscheidung im Rahmen der unternehmerischen Internationalisierung, Wien 1991, p. 67.

9. See Breit, J.: Die Marktselektion im Rahmen der unternehmerischen Internationalisierung, Wien 1991, p. 134.

10. See Ringle, G.: Exportmarketing, Wiesbaden 1977, p. 69.

11. Ciarrapico, A. M.: Country Risk: A Theoretical Framework of Analysis. Dartmouth 1992, p. 4-6.

12. "Österreichs Unternehmer geben sich optimistisch," Handelsblatt Nr. 39, 25. 2. 1992, p. 8.

13. Springer, R.: Neuordnung der internationalen Distributionssysteme der Exportproduzenten der DDR. In: Trommsdorff (Hrsg.): Handelsforschung 1990, Internationalisierung im Handel, Jahrbuch der Forschungsstelle für den Handel Berlin, Wiesbaden 1990, pp. 112.

14. The study "1992 East European Investment Survey" lists in a ranked order the following reasons for investments in Eastern Europe: (1) Establish market shares; (2) Tap regional markets; (3) Low-cost souring; (4) Tap EC market. Business International and Creditanstalt, Vienna, October 1992.

15. The study "1992 East European Investment Survey" indicates in a ranked order the following problem areas (importance and weight of the problem areas are diminishing from the first rank down): (1) Economic environment too uncer-

tain; (2) Political environment too volatile; (3) Finding a suitable partner; (4) Legal system too ambiguous; (5) Negotiating with government authorities; (6) Establishing clear ownership; (7) Lack of physical infrastructure; (8) Valuation; (9) Restructuring costs too high; (10) Environmental liabilities; (11) Clear corporate governance. Business International and Creditanstalt, Vienna, October 1992.

16. For further comments on management in Eastern Europe see Perlaki, I.: "Management Development for Eastern Europe," Multinational Business Review, Spring 1993, pp. 10.

17. See Aaker, D.: Strategisches Marktmanagement, Wiesbaden 1989, pp. 5.

18. See Donutil, H.: "Ungarn: Ohr am Markt," industrie, 10. Dezember 1992, p. 23.

19. Keegan, W. J.: Global Marketing Management, Englewood Cliffs 1989, pp. 24.

20. Kroeber-Riel, W.: Konsumentenverhalten, München 1990, pp. 45 and p. 423.

21. The buying behavior of Polish customers is discussed by Gajewski, S.: Consumer Behavior in Economics of Shortage, Journal of Business Research, Vol. 24, No. 1, January 1992, pp. 5.

22. See Shama, A.: Transforming the Consumer in Russia and Eastern Europe, International Marketing Review, Vol. 9 No. 5, 1992, p. 53.

23. The organisational buying behaviour of Polish companies is discussed by Domanski, T./Guzek, E.: Industrial Buying Behavior: The Case of Poland, Journal of Business Research, Vol. 24, No. 1, January 1992, pp. 11.

24. Kravis, J. B.: Availability and other Influences on the Commodity Composition of Trade, Journal of Economic Policy, Vol. 64, April 1956, pp. 143-155.

25. Berekoven, L.: Internationales Marketing, Herne/Berlin 1985, p. 154.

26. For advertising in Eastern Europe see also Church, N.: Advertising in the Eastern Bloc: Current Practicies and Anticipated Avenues of Development, Journal of Global Marketing, Vol. 5(3) 1992, pp. 109.

27. "Gerade in der Wirtschaftswerbung wird ein sehr starkes Wachstum beobachtet," Handelsblatt, 1993/05/04.

28. Specht, G.: Distributions management, Stuttgart 1988, p. 129.

29. See Iwinska-Knop, K.: Distribution as a Barrier to Application of Marketing in the Centrally Planned Economy (Case Study of Poland), Journal of Business Research, Vol. 24, No. 1, January 1992, pp. 19.

Index

Acquisitions, as market entry mode,
    85,87-88
Advertising, 95,97
Albania
    geopolitical restructuring of, 76
    market attractiveness versus risk
        potential of, 82
    market research data availability
        in, 90
Alcatel, 1
Alcatel SEL, joint venture with
    TESLA Liptovsky Hradok,
    1-16
    employee recruitment and
        training, 8,11,12,13,14,
        15,16
    management organization, 8,9
    market potential, 13-14
    motives of partners, 5,7
    political uncertainty factor, 13
    products, 8,10
    structure, 7-8
Austria
    advertising expenditures in, 98,101
    financial markets in, 39,40
    national bank of, 39,40,45n
    stock market capitalization in, 39
Austrian companies, market entry
        modes of, 83

Bank of Austria, 39,40,45n
Banks
    joint venture financing by, 43
    local, lack of credibility, 41
    national, 39,40,45n
Barter arrangements, 42-43,100
Brand names, global, 42
Brands, development and
        introduction of, 97

Budget reform, 70
Build strategies, joint ventures and,
    87
Bulgaria
    attitudes towards privatization in,
        72
    foreign debt of, 50
    geopolitical restructuring of, 76
    industrial production decrease in,
        39
    market attractiveness versus risk
        potential of, 82
    market opportunities in
        economic background, 50
        factors related to, 61,62,65
        marketing environment and,
        58,59
    market research data availability
        in, 90
    privatization in, 50
Buy-back, 100
Buying behavior
    of consumers, 90-91
    organizational, 91-92,93,94
Buy strategies, privatization and, 87
Belorussia, attitudes towards
        privatization in, 72

Capital, local, lack of, 41
Caron, Pieter, 8,9
Central Europe. *See* Eastern Europe
Centre for Advanced Studies, Kiev,
        Ukraine, 18
Channel management, 98-99
Channel relationships, of markets in
        transition, 23-24
Checklist-method, of market
        selection, 76,77
Clearing-account barter, 100

   105

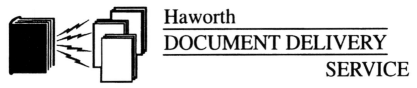

Haworth
DOCUMENT DELIVERY
SERVICE

This valuable service provides a single-article order form for any article from a Haworth journal.

- *Time Saving:* No running around from library to library to find a specific article.
- *Cost Effective:* All costs are kept down to a minimum.
- *Fast Delivery:* Choose from several options, including same-day FAX.
- *No Copyright Hassles:* You will be supplied by the original publisher.
- *Easy Payment:* Choose from several easy payment methods.

Open Accounts Welcome for . . .
- Library Interlibrary Loan Departments
- Library Network/Consortia Wishing to Provide Single-Article Services
- Indexing/Abstracting Services with Single Article Provision Services
- Document Provision Brokers and Freelance Information Service Providers

---

MAIL or *FAX* THIS ENTIRE ORDER FORM TO:

Haworth Document Delivery Service   **or FAX:** 1-800-895-0582
The Haworth Press, Inc.   **or CALL:** 1-800-342-9678
10 Alice Street   9am-5pm EST
Binghamton, NY 13904-1580

PLEASE SEND ME PHOTOCOPIES OF THE FOLLOWING SINGLE ARTICLES:
1) Journal Title: _____
    Vol/Issue/Year:_____ Starting & Ending Pages:_____
Article Title:_____
_____

2) Journal Title: _____
    Vol/Issue/Year:_____ Starting & Ending Pages:_____
Article Title:_____
_____

3) Journal Title: _____
    Vol/Issue/Year:_____ Starting & Ending Pages:_____
Article Title:_____
_____

4) Journal Title: _____
    Vol/Issue/Year:_____ Starting & Ending Pages:_____
Article Title:_____
_____

(See other side for Costs and Payment Information)

COSTS: Please figure your cost to order quality copies of an article.

1. Set-up charge per article: $8.00
   ($8.00 × number of separate articles)   _____

2. Photocopying charge for each article:

   1-10 pages: $1.00   _____

   11-19 pages: $3.00   _____

   20-29 pages: $5.00   _____

   30+ pages: $2.00/10 pages

3. Flexicover (optional): $2.00/article   _____

4. Postage & Handling: US: $1.00 for the first article/
   $.50 each additional article   _____

   Federal Express: $25.00   _____

   Outside US: $2.00 for first article/
   $.50 each additional article _____

5. Same-day FAX service: $.35 per page   _____

GRAND TOTAL: _____

METHOD OF PAYMENT: (please check one)

❑ Check enclosed   ❑ Please ship and bill. PO # _____
   (sorry we can ship and bill to bookstores only! All others must pre-pay)

❑ Charge to my credit card: ❑ Visa; ❑ MasterCard; ❑ Discover;
   ❑ American Express;

Account Number:_____ Expiration date:_____

Signature: *X*_____

Name: _____ Institution: _____

Address: _____

_____

City: _____ State:_____ Zip:_____

Phone Number: _____ FAX Number: _____

MAIL or *FAX* THIS ENTIRE ORDER FORM TO:

Haworth Document Delivery Service	**or FAX:** 1-800-895-0582
The Haworth Press, Inc.	**or CALL:** 1-800-342-9678
10 Alice Street	9am-5pm EST)
Binghamton, NY 13904-1580	